THE SECRETS OF ANCIENT WITCHCRAFT

with

The Witches Tarot

THE SECRETS OF ANCIENT WITCHCRAFT

with

The Witches Tarot

by

ARNOLD AND PATRICIA CROWTHER
with Introduction and Notes by Dr. Leo Louis Martello

A Citadel Press Book
Published by Carol Publishing Group

First Carol Publishing Group Edition 1992

A Citadel Press Book
Published by Carol Publishing Group
Citadel Press is a registered trademark of Carol Communications, Inc.

Editorial Offices: 600 Madison Avenue, New York, NY 10022
Sales & Distribution Offices: 120 Enterprise Avenue, Secaucus, NJ 07094
In Canada: Canadian Manda Group, P.O. Box 920, Station U, Toronto, Ontario, M8Z 5P9, Canada

Queries regarding rights and permissions should be addressed to:
Carol Publishing Group, 600 Madison Avenue, New York, NY 10022

Manufactured in the United States of America
ISBN 0-8065-1056-0

Carol Publishing Group books are available at special discounts for bulk purchases, for sales promotions, fund raising, or educational purposes. Special editions can also be created to specifications. For details contact: Special Sales Department, Carol Publishing Group, 120 Enterprise Ave., Secaucus, NJ 07094

10 9 8 7 6 5 4 3

Contents

THE SECRETS OF ANCIENT WITCHCRAFT

with

The Witches Tarot

Introduction

DR. LEO LOUIS MARTELLO
Author of *Witchcraft: The Old Religion*

Arnold and Patricia Crowther are among England's most famous Witch couples. She is a dancer-actress; he is a professional stage magician. Several years ago Arnold introduced Patricia to Gerald Gardner, who initiated her into Witchcraft. She in turn initiated Arnold. When they got married Dr. Gardner flew in from the Isle of Man to perform the Witches' handfasting ceremony. Later they had a civil ceremony. The marriage was highly publicized in the English press.

The Crowthers have written the book *The Witches Speak*, introduced to Americans by this writer. Patricia has also written *Witch Blood: The Autobiography of a Witch High Priestess*, with an Introduction by myself. She wrote a documentary for British radio, *A Spell of Witchcraft*, and has appeared on numerous radio and television programs in England.

Unlike many of the *nouveau Witches* who master

7

their own rituals but do little research on their own, the Crowthers are relentless in their constant search for the "fragments of a forgotten faith." Although technically they may be called "Gardnerians," they refer to themselves as Witches, stating that the term "Gardnerian" was originated only after Gardner had died. Patricia was one of the Witch heirs mentioned in Gardner's will.

Although I have been initiated into four other Witchcraft traditions besides my own, this is the first time that I am revealing my initiation into the Gardnerian branch. Because I have always insisted on retaining my independence, I have neither sought nor wanted initiation into the Gardnerian tradition as practised in the United States. When I agreed to undergo this initiation it was because I respected the High Priestess and High Priest involved: Patricia and Arnold Crowther. I also respect their loyalty to the late Gerald Gardner,. though I don't always agree with them. Further, I preferred to get my information firsthand from the Crowthers rather than secondhand from American Gardnerians who never met Gardner. I did go to a newly initiated High Priest and asked for a Gardnerian initiation from his newly initiated High Priestess (without revealing my prior initiation) just to test them and to confirm an intuition. However, I could not reconcile myself to certain things they were doing and felt it was necessary to "get out from under" by revealing that I, too, am an initiated Gardnerian Witch and produced proof of same. I enjoyed the spectacle of watching some of these *nouveau Gardnerians* acting as though they possessed the "Holy Grail" secrets! The Crowthers never reveal the names of those who belong to their coven, and most of the coven members don't even know each other's real names. In this way they practice the true Craft as put forth in the *Book Of Shadows*: "So be it ardane that no coven shall know where the next coven abide, or who its members be, save only the priestess and priest, and the messenger. And there shall be no communication between them, save by the messenger of the Gods, or the summoner, and only if it be safe may the covens meet in some safe place for the great festivals. And while there, none may say whence they came nor tell their true names. To this and that, if any are tortured, in their agony they may not tell if they do not know."

In this book the Crowthers write: "We certainly know that Aleister Crowley never wrote any rituals for Witches. Covens are governed by a High Priestess, and Crowley was not the kind of person to be bossed about by women." The last part is true but it does not negate the first part. With all due respect to them, in the rite known as "Drawing Down The Moon" there is this passage from "The Gnostic Mass" in Crowley's *Magick in Theory and Practice*: "Therefore by seed and root, and stem and bud, And leaf and flower and fruit do we invoke thee." There are other instances. It is well known that Gardner knew Crowley and that Crowley gave him an *Ordo Templi Orientis* (O.T.O.) Charter (which Gardner never used but exhibited at his Museum of Witchcraft on the Isle of Man. In *Witch Blood* Patricia tells about her own meeting with Crowley just before his demise.

In a letter to me, dated October 14, 1973, Patricia Crowther writes: "It seems there is much wrong thinking about Gerald and his people. He was initiated into a hereditary group in the New Forest, and we have met some of the people from this group. Doreen

Valiente has also met some of them, and was herself initiated by Gardner. The idea of 'Gardnerians' was introduced by two men, one of whom I worked with in one of Gerald's covens; the other has since died. They tried to imply that they were something different, that is, hereditary. This is nonsense as the Wicca believe in reincarnation, which owes nothing to genetic lineage. Of course, there are people who have gained knowledge through their own families, but even in the old days, people were brought in, otherwise the Craft would not have survived."

My hereditary Witch friends disagree with the Crowthers and others who were brought into the Craft by Gerald Gardner. One of them, William Liddell, who now lives in Auckland, New Zealand, has told me that the Gardnerians bring certain things into the circle that the hereditary Witches never would. In "Thoughts On the Third Degree" an article I wrote for the periodical, No. 59 *Green Egg*, I said: "The Gardnerian, Alexandrian and Neo-Gardnerian groups (including many who call themselves Traditional) have a system of three degrees. A number of authors claim that Gardner was initiated into a Traditional coven; a few have said that it was Hereditary. It may have been Traditional but it most emphatically was *not* Hereditary. The Hereditary English Witches did not—do not—have degrees and they do *not* call the admission of a neophyte an initiation. They also do *not* use many of the Witch implements propagated by Gardner and would not bring certain things into the Circle. (They also do not use this term). Furthermore, unlike the Gardnerian *Book Of Shadows* (and its derivatives) which says: "And it is for this reason that a man may be taught by a woman and a woman by a man, and that woman and woman and man and man should never attempt these practices together." In some versions there is added: "And may the curse of the Mighty Ones be on any who make such an attempt." In Hereditary covens the Magister could initiate both men and women.

In Doreen Valiente's *An ABC Of Witchcraft* she discusses Gardner's meeting Aleister Crowley, whom he "admired as a poet, and was fond of using quotations from Crowley's works in his rites." She also says that "the Craft consists of three degrees. It would be out of place for me to go into more detail. However, on the other hand there are references from old sources, which state that witchcraft consisted of three degrees of initiation; and G. B. G. in his writings has referred to the resemblances between some features of Masonic initiation, and some features of Witch initiations. He has stated his belief that there has been in the past some definite connection between these two traditions, a belief which he bases upon these resemblances."

Valiente points out the similarities between Masonry and Witchcraft but does not cite "the references from old sources" indicating three degrees in Witchcraft. In *Discoverie of Witchcraft*, the author Reginald Scot, says that a Witch goes through "three admission ceremonies." That is quite a different thing than "three degrees," though it may be used to justify the latter. It is like the attorney who had to take his bar examination three times because he failed the first two. On the third he passed and was admitted (licensed) as a practising attorney. Degrees imply high status based on merit: elementary school, high school and then college; or, as I wrote in *Green Egg*: "The three degree system provokes status seeking. It is as though first is high, second is higher and third is highest. A priest is not a bishop and a bishop is not a cardinal and a cardinal is not the Pope! If there is a degree system then there should be rational and ethical standards by which they are given based on merit." I concluded this article with "I am not trying to undermine those who use it but merely trying to point out some of the psychological—emotional reactions that they often provoke." In the final analysis I still prefer a first-rate person more than I do a third-degree Witch."

In my own book *Witchcraft: The Old Religion,* I write about Gardner in the chapter "Pioneers of Witchcraft's New Renaissance." The two other pioneers were Charles Godfrey Leland, whose *Aradia, or Gospel of the Witches* was published in 1899, and Margaret A. Murray, whose *Witch Cult In Western Europe* came out in 1921. Gardner's first book, under the penname *Scire* was published in 1949, followed by *Witchcraft Today* in 1954. Some thought that I was too critical in what I wrote, but my comments were based on information from his own writings, and a biography by Jack Bracelin, as well as from others who knew him in those days, including two who had participated with him in the early covens. I concluded the chapter by saying, "Gerald B. Gardner's books are must reading for all those sincerely interested in the Craft. Despite his faults, he singlehandedly brought the Old Religion to the forefront of public attention—something viewed with horror by its more traditional diehards—and this has been both good and bad. Since his demise, thousands of books have been written on witchcraft, most of them worthless, but the truth has also gotten through and inspired others to do research on their own."

Unlike most Tarot decks, which seem to be variations on a theme, the Witches' Tarot presented here is totally Craft oriented. The vaguely Christian trappings depicted on most decks have been eliminated and replaced by genuine Wicca symbolism. There is a feeling for the old ways, and the symbolisms recapture our pagan past. The male and female figures are skyclad (nude) in keeping with Gardnerian tradition and the passage in Leland's *Aradia* which says, "as the sign that ye are truly free, ye shall be naked in your rites." Even though many Hereditary and Traditional Witches deny that nudity was an essential part of their rites, especially in the British Isles, whose climate was most unsuitable for skyclad worship, unlike the warmer climate of the Mediterranean where the Italian Witches of *Aradia* could do so comfortably, the nudity depicted in these cards represents a healthy attitude towards the body and sex. As befitting a fertility, and nature-oriented earth religion where sex was considered sacred, the Witches Tarot is frankly sensual and devoid of the clothed, guilty hang-ups of Judeo-Christian theology. The only fully clothed figure is that of The Fool depicted as a Christian priest or minister.

As I point out in my book *Understanding The Tarot*, the origin of the Tarot is shrouded in mystery, and I give the various explanations of its derivations. In Idries Shah's *The Sufis*, he says that the Tarot cards were introduced into the West in 1379, and quotes the chronicler Feliciano Busi: "In the year 1379 was brought into Viterbo the game of cards, which comes from Saracina and is called by them *Naib*." Shah explains that *Naib* is an Arabic word meaning "deputy" and that these cards are substitutional material, an allegory, of a Sufi master. *Naib* is divided into four sections called *turug* (four ways) and undoubtedly the word from which Tarot is derived. The Spanish word *naipe* (card) may stem from the Arabic *naib*. In *It's In The Cards* I wrote: "It is almost certain that playing cards were introduced to Europe via Spain by the Arabs and Moors. They were called *naibi:* The Arabic and Hebrew words *nabi, naba,* and *nabaa* mean "to foretell." Idries Shah's *The Sufis* was published in 1964, the same year in which my own *It's in the Cards* came out, and which I received the summer that I was living in Tangier, Morocco, trying to research the Tarot at the University of Fez.

Idries Shah's most interesting passage on the Tarot is:

> The Tarot now known to the West has been influenced by a Cabalistic and Judaizing process designed to bring it into line with certain doctrines not implicit in the original. Superficial attempts to link these cards with those in Persia or China have not succeeded because the essential cipher elements contained in the meanings of the suits and the trumps is still a Sufi property. The pack, as it stands today, is only partially correct, because there have been transpositions of the significances of some of the *atouts,* the trumps or emblematic figures on the pack. This error has been caused by a mistranslation from Arabic of certain words, due to literal conversion into a different culture system. Another factor may be substitution of one picture for another one. This is not a subject upon which I may be much more explicit. Temperance is incorrectly portrayed and interpreted; so is the fifteenth trump; the meaning of the sixteenth

trump is a classic case of misunderstanding of a word; the twentieth is wrongly emphasized. Many of the attributions, however, are still in use among the Sufis, though in the West the essential associations with Sufi texts have been lost.

In most Tarot decks Temperance is illustrated with an "angel" pouring water or wine from one cup to another. In the Witches' Tarot, modelled after other such decks, but whose symbolisms are totally Wicca, this card shows a naked woman pouring a libation from one drinking *horn* into another. The fifteenth card which Shah says is incorrectly portrayed in most Tarot decks—as The Devil—is here depicted as Baphomet, and closer to the representation of the Horned God. Shah says that the twentieth card in regular Tarot decks is "wrongly emphasized." It is usually depicted by an archangel blowing a trumpet, with various men and women arising from their coffins. In the Witches Tarot it is simply called Rebirth and its symbolism is joyous in contrast to the somberness depicted in most Tarot decks. The Witches Tarot is at least true to its own symbolism, and I daresay closer to the original Sufi meanings than the other Tarot decks which show a strong Judeo-Christian influence. Then, too, there is a belief among Witches that their origins stem from the East.

One need only read the answers to the various questions asked of the Crowthers in the second part of the book, *A Witch Under Fire*, to see that they are rational people who don't fit the stereotyped image of Witches fostered by the Church and promoted by a sensationalist press. Like myself, they maintain a steely detachment from all the nonsense that passes itself off as the occult, witchcraft and the supernatural. As a professional magician, Arnold Crowther knows the "tricks of the trade" practised by fraudulent materialization mediums, and Patricia Crowther has always been cool under fire. Our views are basically compatible when it comes to self-styled Satanists or Black Magicians. We consider them to be mediocrities out to impress, whose power is never demonstrated in any kind of tangible achievement, and who parasitically need people more insecure than themselves to sustain them in their self-delusion of using "magick" to harm others. The only power that these charlatans have is the power given to them by those who have abandoned their own thinking processes and accepted the views, opinions and unproven assertions of others. Their weakness provides the strength for these so-called Black Arts Practitioners. Like one prison inmate who recently corresponded with a woman interested in the Old Religion, whom he contacted via her listing in the *Wica Newsletter*, and who insisted that the Horned God was really the Devil, and who called himself a "Satanic Warlock." When this woman wrote back that they were philosophically incompatible, and that she would terminate the correspondence, the prison inmate threatened to "work against her." I wrote her: "If he had any kind of power just what the hell is he doing in jail?"

Reading this book one must remember that it is written by two Witches originally initiated by Gerald Gardner, although they have also been initiated into a Scotch Hereditary group with whom they work closely. When it became known that I too was initiated into this branch of the Craft some of these "Gardnerians" gave it more importance than even I did, even

going so far as to express doubt! My English Hereditary Witch-friends either shrugged or were amused.
They know both the Crowthers and Doreen Valiente
and all the others who have become known but they
are strictly underground and have never admitted their
Craft affiliation to others not of their own tradition.
. . . with one exception, myself. They gave me a 100
page manuscript to be used in a future book showing
the differences among the Hereditary Witches and all
the other traditions.

Readers of this book who want to learn more
about Witchcraft and the Old Religion, and who would
like to receive a Recommended Old Religion Book List,
and a Coven-Craft Application form, should send a
self-addressed stamped envelope to me: Dr. Leo Louis
Martello, Suite 1B, 153 West 80th Street, New York,
N.Y. 10024.

NOTE: Arnold Crowther passed away, after a long
illness, and many operations, on May 1, 1974. He died in
Patricia's arms.

PART I

The Green Goddess

The goddess of the Witches has had many names. So many, in fact, that she is often called the Nameless One.

As she was the Great Mother of all living things, and Goddess of Land and Sea, the ancients saw her everywhere—in the woods and forests, in the hills and in the flowering countryside.

Her reign covered the summer season of the year; from the time when the vegetation began to turn green and the trees began to bud.

When the leaves turned brown and began to fall, she returned to the summerlands of the gods, where she rested until her rebirth the following spring.

The Horned God of Death and Hunting took over from her on Halloween, and ruled during the winter months.

The ancients knew her as the Green Goddess.

1

The Ancient Rite of Initiation

Modern witchcraft ceremonies have altered a great deal from those of ancient times. During the ages, many things have been added and altered, perhaps to keep up with the times, or through the infiltration of people from other cults. This sort of change is bound to happen when rituals are passed down by word of mouth and nothing is in writing. The fact that in witchcraft there is no governing body, and that each group of witches is autonomous, also gives an opening for variations in the rites.

Other religions have suffered in the same way as witchcraft, and one can hardly believe that Tibetan Buddhism and Zen Buddhism have anything to do with the original teachings of Buddha. Christianity has followed the same growth, and the variations of the different sects are far too numerous to discuss.

Modern witches are the survival of the priesthood of the ancient craft. The priests were the people who performed the rites within the circle while the worshipers sat outside like the congregation of a church. This is the difficulty with the modern craft and the reason why genuine witches turn away so many of the people who seek to join. If one could hold ceremonies in the stone circles of olden times it would be possible to get a lot more followers. So many of the people who seek initiation are unsuitable for the priesthood but would be all right as worshipers of the old gods.

The disadvantage of holding such a meeting would be the vandals and troublemakers who always seem to turn up on such occasions and try to break up the proceedings. This is what happens when the Druids hold their festivals at Stonehenge.

My wife, Patricia, and I once discussed with the police the idea of holding an open meeting at one of the stone circles in Derbyshire. They said there would be no objection from them, but that at the present time we would only be asking for trouble from Mods, Rockers and Skinheads, and the police had all they could cope with at football matches and with student demonstrations. They preferred that people not stick their necks out by doing things that might attract such gangs.

In modern witch rites, we find terms and expressions that are also used in Masonry, the Golden Dawn and other such occult societies; but it is difficult to say if the witches took over terms from these people or if the societies adopted them from the witches.

We certainly know that Aleister Crowley never wrote any rituals for witches. Covens are governed by a high priestess, and Crowley was not the kind of person who would be bossed about by women.

To understand the ancient rite of initiation, one must go back to prehistoric times. The first deity of Britain was female—a mother goddess—and the reason for this is very understandable. Everybody knew it was the female that gave birth, both in the human and animal kingdoms; so according to logic, the creator must be a woman. Mother Nature was born and the people began to worship the Goddess of Magic and Fertility.

Man knew that he produced the "seed" from his own body, but he needed the magical body of the female to develop the seed and turn it into a human being, as well as to suckle the infant with milk from her own breasts until it could fend for itself. Prehistoric people also thought that if the female could work such great magic as producing life, she must be able to use the magic power from her body for other purposes. This caused her to become the leader of the tribe's magic rites and the priestess of the earliest religion. Those women who carried out the rituals were initiated into the feminine priesthood and, in years to come, would become the witches or wise ones.

Early man saw the Great Mother in the whole of nature. Hills and mountains represented her breasts, and caves symbolized her womb. Anything that faintly resembled the genital organs of a woman, like a cleft stick, an oval, a cowrie shell, or a stone with a hole through it became a symbol of the Goddess.

Women who were initiated into the female priesthood had to be reborn in the womb of the Great Mother. A cave was used for this purpose, especially one with a long passage leading into a chamber. Wookey Hole, in Somerset, England, is one such cave, and was certainly used for initiations. It also has its legend of the Witch of Wookey, which may have come down to us from folk-memory. The legend has, of course, been Christianized, and the Abbot of Glastonbury is said to have turned the witch into stone by sprinkling her with holy water. A stalagmite in the cave is said to be the witch turned into stone. If this is so, then she must have been a giant, for the stalagmite is some twenty feet high. With a great effort of imagination, one can visualize a cloaked and hooded figure. An ancient skeleton of a woman, along with a crude crystal ball, was discovered in the cave; this may have been the priestess who was in charge of this sacred place. The crystal ball suggests that she was also a kind of oracle.

In those early days, the sex act was not frowned upon as something evil and only spoken about in whispers. It was considered as natural an act as eating and drinking. One must remember that early man, being nude, would not have had the same sex urge as people wearing clothes. Clothes were invented chiefly to attract the opposite sex, and not to ward off the cold as most people imagine. Prehistoric folk were acclimatized to all sorts of weather, and it was only after the introduction of clothes that people became sensitive to changes of climate.

Man copied the idea of dressing up to attract the female from the animals and birds. When Stone Age man realized that the males of most species had some colorful adornment that was displayed during the mating season, he began to adorn himself with feathers, bangles and other trinkets, hoping that the females of the tribe would be attracted by them.

Later, as rivalry grew, men added more decorations to his body, like the tattoo. One thing led to another, and man began dressing up in animal skins, believing that in doing so he also took on the power of that animal whose skin he wore. Thus clothes were invented. This not only produced the mystery of what was behind the garments, but the friction of the material itself against the sensitive sexual organs helped to increase man's sexual desires.

Nudity is perhaps the most antisexual condition there is, and anyone who has attended a nudist club will confirm this. In prehistoric times, it must have oeen even worse than today. There was not much difference in the appearance of one Stone Age man and another; they all had long hair, full beards, and extremely hairy bodies. The latter also applied to Stone Age woman. One would not have found attractive women, complete with makeup and smooth skin, like the women depicted in modern films about the period. In order for tribes to survive, the members had to try and make themselves attractive to each other, for which purpose ornaments of bone and other materials were used. This is still done in "primitive" tribes of the present day, and decorations that we consider ugly, like stretching the lips with wooden disks, or tattooing the face with blue symbols, are thought to enhance the beauty of the natives. One cannot judge other people by our own standards, and the saying "beauty is in the eyes of the beholder" is very true.

There is little doubt that the earliest human beings, like animals, had a breeding season. This was around springtime, when all religious festivals took place to herald the new year and when vegetation began to awaken from its long winter sleep. The saying "in spring a young man's fancy turns to thoughts of love," comes down to us from folk memory. If this was not the case, why should one time of the year be more favorable to lovers than any other?

In the old initiation ceremony, the priestesses knew exactly how a child was conceived and born, and as it was a fertility religion, to be reborn in the circle meant having to undergo a ritual that was symbolic of a real birth. This was a case of sympathetic magic. The initiate represented the seed of man, and, first of all, had to be thrust into the vagina of the Great Mother, which was symbolized by the passage that led into the chamber of the cave.

Ancient ceremonies had very few verbal rites, as actions were thought to be more important. It was easier and simpler for an initiate to remember what she had gone through than to remember a lot of words.

First, her hands were tied behind her back, and then she was bound up in a crouching position so that she resembled an embryo in a prenatal position. Vines or platted reeds were used for the binding, since rope or cord had not been invented.

The rest of the women lined up two abreast, and the initiate was hoisted above the heads of the first four or six women, depending upon the size and weight of the initiate. The procession then marched to the entrance of the cave. This double line of females represented the male phallus.

Slowly the procession entered the passage of the cave until it arrived at the entrance of the chamber, which symbolized the womb. There it halted, and the whole line of females began to rock backward and forward, symbolizing the rhyhmic movement of the sex act. At the word of the priestess in command, the initiate was cast into the chamber; this was the climax of the act—the ejaculation of the semen into the womb. This was done, regardless of any injury she might receive from her fall. There she remained for twenty-four hours, or as near to a whole day and night that could be judged in those days. The period of lying in the dark represented the time it took for the seed to grow into a baby. It also produced the fear and suffering that must always precede initiation.

All the initiate could do was to lie and meditate and hope to survive all the horrors that might come to a person who was left bound in a cave. Bats would flutter by, and often got entangled in her hair; other nocturnal creatures scampered over her body. Beasts of prey could easily wander in and devour her, or she might die of fright or exposure. Sometimes, a few of the other women would dress in skins and prowl about the initiate, making animal sounds to terrify her. If she died, owing to fright or some other cause, the death symbolized a miscarriage, and showed that she was unworthy to become a priestess and had been rejected by the Goddess.

When the required time had elapsed, and the initiate had successfully passed the test, the rest of the women entered the cave. Four carried torches, which they stuck in the ground at the four points of the compass, thus lighting up the cavern. A circle was scratched on the floor of the cave, around the initiate, with a hazel stick wand, and the Goddess was called upon to witness the rite. When all this was completed, those present joined hands and ran around the circle, going faster and faster until they dropped from exhaustion. This dance raised the Witches' power, and symbolically represented the quickening of the womb, which the circle portrayed. Even Shakespeare spoke of a woman's genital organ as the "circle."

Now was the time for the initiate to be reborn into a new life, as she had overcome the fear of loneliness and darkness. The rest of the women stood, one behind the other, with their legs apart, each holding the waist of the one in front. The space between their legs represented the triangle of rebirth, and the tunnel thus formed symbolized the vagina.

Still bound and suffering from cramps from being tied up for so long, the initiate was made to struggle through the tunnel of legs. As she slowly passed through, the rest of the women moaned and groaned, imitating a pregnant woman in labor. The way in which the initiate struggled through was looked upon as an easy or a difficult birth.

When the initiate finally made her way through the tunnel, she was lifted up and her bonds cut. This symbolized the cutting of the umbilical cord; the severed bonds were presented to her for later use in working magic.

The priestess in charge then offered her breasts to the newly born priestess, as a mother offers her milk to a newly born babe. This ritual was repeated by all the other women to show that each accepted the new member of the priesthood as if she were her own child and would protect her as a mother would.

The initiate was then purified by taking a ritual bath in a nearby stream or, if there was one, in a pool in the cave. In places devoid of caves, the ritual would be conducted in a wood clearing or some other hollow spot. Later, man-made circles, with or without stones, were constructed in sacred places dedicated to the Great Mother.

On the top of the hill, above the chalk figure of the Long Man of Wilmington, in Sussex, England, there is the remains of such a circle. It is surrounded by a mound, with an entrance at the south; at the north, stand two man-made hillocks. The mound and the hillocks represent the womb and breasts of the Great Mother. In Ireland, there are two round hills next to each other, with a prehistoric stone circle at the base of them. These hills are known as the Paps of Anu,* one of the old Celtic names of the Goddess. It is obvious that this was an old place of initiation and worship.

The many ancient barrows that are spread over England symbolize the dead being returned to the womb of Mother Earth: they were buried in the prenatal position so that they could be reborn again. In ancient Egypt, the same idea was used, but pyramids replaced the hills and caves. The famous Great Pyramid, near Cairo, however, was used for initiations, never for burials. The pyramid shape represents the female pubic triangle, the entrance passage represents the vagina, and the inner chamber symbolizes the womb. All pyramids are dedicated to the Goddess Isis, who is another form of the Great Mother.

The priestesses of the old religion remained virgins and dedicated their lives to the Goddess. The power that would have been used for begetting children was used for working magic.

* Anu here is a variation of Annu, also known as Annis, and Danu, the great Irish Mother Goddess and not to be confused with the Babylonian God Anu, supreme in the triad with Enlil and Ea, considered ruler of Heaven and father of Gods.

Like many native tribes, prehistoric man would not deflower a virgin, as menstrual blood was considered unclean and taboo. Even today in some Eastern countries, a woman, during her period, is kept away from the tribe for the same reason.

The ordinary maidens, who would cohabit with males and bear children for the tribe, were taken into the circle and ritually deflowered by the priestess, who used a sacred knife for the purpose. This knife was originally made of flint and was, perhaps, the origin of the athame, or witches' knife, which is used to draw and open the Circle, and which could easily have been handed down from ancient times as a symbol of the rite of "opening the womb."

Later, this rite was known as the "sacrifice of the virgin," and was regarded as a blood sacrifice; it was the source of rumors that virgins were sacrificed in pagan rites.

When men entered the craft, and the Horned God of Hunting was thought to be the chief diety of the witches; it is said that an imitation phallus representing the God was substituted for the knife, and that the virgin sacrificed her virginity to the God instead of the Goddess.

When the Church turned the Horned God into the Christian Devil, tales were circulated that witches were raped by Satan, who used a false phallus. These stories were obviously exaggerations of the ancient rite of deflowering.

After this defloration ceremony, the high priestess covered a small pot with a leaf and pushed the girl's finger through it, symbolizing that the girl's hymen had been broken, and that there would be no danger for any man who wished to copulate with her. The leaf was given to the maiden, who would fasten it around her neck so that the men of the tribe would know that she was now able to become a mother. This leaf was the forerunner of the wedding ring (which was originally made of iron), and the male placed his finger through it. By this act the bride showed that she was ready to give her body to the groom for fertilization. Later, this custom was considered too earthy, and was replaced by the present practice in which the groom places the ring on the bride's third finger. It was once believed that a vein from this finger ran straight to the heart.

2

Hair as an Aid to Magic

According to Henri de Heir, a 16th century writer, pubic hair and hair from the armpits was used for medicinal and pharmaceutical purposes. Hair from the pubes and armpits was stitched into little silk bags and given by young women to their sweethearts as love tokens. This gift was said to be an infallible method of keeping lovers faithful and devoted. The custom still exists today in many parts of Europe.

Proof of this practice comes to me from a woman who lived in Spain prior to World War II. The woman found out that her husband was carrying on an affair, and was advised to consult an old woman who had the reputation of being a witch. The lady in question visited the old woman and discussed her problem.

After hearing the story, the "witch" told my informant that she needed a special love charm in order to bring her husband back. The old woman took a small cloth bag and put into it several herbs; she then asked her client to cut some of the hair from her armpits. The witch was told that this was impossible as the woman always shaved under her arms.

The old witch was horrified and told my friend that she should never do that as she lost a great deal of her power by this act. My friend laughed, and then realized that the old woman was very serious: "It is no laughing matter," the old woman said. "I can do nothing more for you. Come back to me when the hair has grown again. Your stupid act has most probably lost you your husband."

The interview really worried my informant, so she let her underarm hair grow again. In the meantime, she delved into the matter. She noticed that none of the peasant women shaved, and also remembered that her own mother never did either. She came up with the following information: Shaving under the arms was a comparatively new idea that only came to the fore when safety razors were invented. Thus, she presumed that to attempt to shave under the arms with an open, or "cutthroat," razor would not only have been rather difficult, but also dangerous. Businesses commercialized on the new craze, and many makes of hair-removing creams appeared on the market.

She further presumed that the danger of cutting oneself caused the women of previous ages to retain their underarm hair, but found that this was not the reason. Hair in the armpits, or "shade" as it used to be called, was considered one of the more erotic parts of the female body. In fact, it was considered much more sexually attractive than women's breasts, which were often partly exposed, and in some periods were completely naked. Even in my own childhood, women thought nothing of breast-feeding their babies in public. The sight of a naked breast did not excite the average male, but underarm hair did. It was rather like a preview of what one could expect to find on the private parts of a woman.

Charles Dickens, .in *The Pickwick Papers*, described Mr. Pickwick's journey by coach and how the poor man got very annoyed because the baby behind him, on its mother's knee, continued to howl. Pickwick casually turned around and shouted: "Give it the breast woman!" Robert Burns, the Scottish bard, wrote several bawdy poems celebrating a "hairy c---," but ignored female breasts completely.

The short-sleeve dresses of older periods obscured the view of underarm hair, but girls who were out to attract fellows would cunningly raise their arms and expose the hair, knowing the sexual effect it would have on their admirers.

After a couple of months, my friend revisited the old witch, who was then able to complete the love charm. According to my informer, it worked—her husband came back and never left her again. She also declared that by retaining the hair in her armpits, it caused him to become more sexually attracted to her.

In modern witchcraft, the "downward" triangle is said to symbolize the two breasts and the pubic triangle, but in the ancient craft it symbolized the three places on a female body where hair grows—under each arm and in the pubic region.

In ancient manuscripts, to take the power from a witch one was advised to catch her and shave the hair from her armpits. This was believed to stop her from having power over evil spirits, since the hair gave her the power to control the spirits, and because as long as she retained the hair, she had no fear of them.

In many places, this hair is a remedy against evil spirits; in the Aru Islands, for example, men, women and children wear charms and amulets to banish sickness and bad spirits. The amulets consist of little bags that contain such tabooed objects as phallic-shaped pebbles; pearls; animals' gallstones; and under-arm hair from women. Why not pubic hair? The female must willingly supply the hair; and though pubic hair could easily be cut from a female while she was asleep, one could not get hair from her armpits without waking her.

Many societies believe that exposure of the genital organs will exorcise demons. It is a very profound and archaic custom, and was even practiced by Martin Luther, who was tormented by nightly suggestions and visions of Satan. Luther knew no other means of self-defense except to expose his genital organs and buttocks. This practice is often carried out in various parts of the world when death occurs, as ghosts are believed to be frightened of naked bodies. The act is thought to have led to ritual nudity. One of the reasons that witches work naked in the circle is to keep evil entities away, and rituals performed in the nude are freer from troublesome elementals than those per-formed in robes or some other form of dress.

In some parts of the world, sorceresses dye their pubic hair bright red because this is supposed to add greatly to their power to scare away evil spirits. In parts of Germany, it was said that a witch could be recognized by the excess of hair under her arms, and that by raising them and showing it, she could exorcise evil spirits, frighten away ghosts or bewitch people. Such hair was sought after for making charms against evil powers. I was told that some of these witches made charms from their own hair and sold them. In Germany, during the war, I was shown a bracelet made by a witch out of hair from her armpits. It was certainly a work of art and must have taken a great deal of time and patience. I offered to buy it, but the person who owned it refused to sell. He said it was much too powerful a charm to part with.

The first thing those who found witches did was to shave the bodies of their victims, supposedly to find "devil marks," or hidden teats by which witches suckled their familiars. But the witch-finders really believed that a witch's power resided in her body hair. Millaeus witnessed the torture of some women at Toulouse, from whom no confessions could be wrung until they were completely shaven. After this was done, they readily acknowledged the truth of the charge. One woman, who apparently led a pious life, was tortured on suspicion of witchcraft, but bore her agonies with incredible constancy—until complete depilation made her admit her guilt.

The noted inquisitors Sprenger and Cumanus shaved the whole bodies of forty-seven women before having them burned. The English witch-finders had authority for this rigorous scrutiny since Satan, himself, in a sermon he preached from the pulpit of North Berwick Church, comforted his servants by assuring them that no harm could befall them as long as their body hair remained. Satan, in this instance, was the leader of the coven, whom outsiders believed to be the Devil, so it is quite obvious that the witches themselves believed in the power connected with body hair.

Sorcerers and magicians in all countries have sought to get hair from their victims, together with fingernails, spittle or threads of the person's garments, so that they could work their magic against them. Having obtained these objects, the sorcerers chanted spells and curses over them, and then buried them in the ground; as the things decayed, the victim slowly wasted away.

When an Australian Aborigine wishes to get rid of his wife, he cuts off some of her pubic hair when she is asleep and ties it to his spear. He then goes to a neighboring tribe and gives the spear to a friend, who sticks it in the ground every night before the camp fire. When the spear falls down, it is a sign that the wife is dead.

Some students of the occult have read in the story of Samson and Delilah an allegory connecting the loss of body hair with the loss of power. Such stories, they believe, were handed down so that the secret of working magic by the use of body hair would not be entirely lost, and so that future students of the art would be able to glean the real meaning behind the tale.

It has been suggested that many Eastern societies demand that their women remove all body hair to prevent them from holding power over the males. This may be true, as in places where the custom prevails, the women are usually treated like chattel.

Aristophanes tells us that in Hellas, depilation was practiced mainly by brothel prostitutes, but that it later spread to the women of the upper classes. In Rome, some women resorted to depilation in order to make them appear younger than they were, but the

majority of the Roman matrons refused to have anything to do with the practice.

The Koran regarded all people ceremoniously im-
pure who did not shave their bodies, and tells how
King Solomon refused to copulate with Bilkese, Queen
of Sheba, until she had removed all her body hair.
Legend tells us that the queen's silken pubic veil
extended to her knees. This seems somewhat exaggerated, but there must have been such cases, because in
the Sudan women are said to be held in great respect if
their pubic veil extends to their knees. Solomon, being
a magician himself, obviously knew about the magic
power associated with body hair, and, no doubt,
demanded depilation to diminish the queen's power
rather than to facilitate congress.

In England, one of the old country defenses
against witchcraft was the use of the "witch bottle."
When a man believed he was being bewitched, he took
a bottle, filled it with some of his own hair, nail parings
and urine, and placed it on the fire. When it exploded,
the witch was supposed to die, or at least the spell
would be broken. Sometimes these bottles were hung
inside the chimneys of old cottages to protect the
inhabitants against witchcraft. Sometimes such bottles turn up in antique shops, and are quickly bought
up by collectors.

Female hair has always been considered a power
for working magic. One example of this is the length of
platted hair attached to the death-pointing bones of the
Australian Aborigines. The power to cause death is
believed to come from this hair, and the bone is just
the instrument for directing this power. The most
powerful pointing bone is made from the forearm of a
dead woman. To the blunt end of the bone is attached a

cord of finely braided human hair—a woman's hair. The cord is about a yard long, and is cemented to the bone by a resinous substance which resembles pitch. It comes from the spinifex bush, and is obtained by burning dried spinifex. When the fire has died down, the ash is blown away and the residue kneaded into a small black pliable ball. The hair is attached to the bone while the substance is warm, and becomes very hard when the substance cools. These bones are said to be extremely deadly in the hands of a skilled magician.

When the bone is completed, the killer goes off into the bush, where he sits in a ritual position and points the bone in the direction of his intended victim. While doing this, he jerks the bone backward and forward while he sings a chant to it. One such chant has been translated as follows:

> May your heart be rent asunder.
> May your backbone be split open
> and your ribs torn asunder.
> May your head and throat be split open.

This is believed to send forth a kind of "shadow" bone into the victim's body. The bone is then burned and the chant sung again. This causes the ghost bone to pierce the victim's heart, and he will slowly die.

It is generally known that combing the hair produces a certain amount of electricity, but more powerful electricity (or whatever you like to call it) can be generated by combing pubic or underarm hair. Even stroking it softly will raise this power, and this was one of the techniques the ancients used for working magic.

In the beginning of this century, body hair was considered unsightly and "not quite nice," an attitude which caused many women to depilate themselves. Men have never favored this and are not embarrassed at showing underarm hair. Was this some subtle method of keeping women powerless?

Recently, with women taking a prominent part in sports, with the innovation of nudist clubs, and now, with the Women's Lib Movement, females are beginning to care little what their straight-laced sisters thought about body hair and just leave it. It is as natural a part of the body as eyebrows. As women are now becoming more liberated, it may be the magic in their hair working.

3

Sex Magick

It is fairly certain that witchcraft was originally a woman's cult. If we assume that our prehistoric ancestors were similar to the people of present-day primitive tribes which have not altered through the centuries, we can presume that both sexes had their own secret societies or cults into which members of the opposite sex were not allowed.

We have two dieties of the witches—the Mother Goddess and the Horned God—so it is not difficult to believe that the God was worshiped by the men, who were hunters, and that the Goddess belonged to the women, who did most of the early agricultural work.

In those early days, neither the sex act nor masturbation was frowned upon; they were just pleasant pastimes—gifts from the gods. Very early man had no idea that he had anything to do with childbirth, and presumed that it was purely a magical act that could only be performed by women. Even the females had no idea that males had anything to do with it, and would lie naked in the moonlight so that the moon deity would cause them to become pregnant.

This state of affairs did not last very long, and people slowly discovered that a member of each sex was needed in order to produce new life. From this time, male semen was regarded as a magical substance, and hunters used to masturbate over their weapons in order to consecrate them, thus giving them life and making them more powerful. Certain Arab tribes continued to do this with their daggers, and, for all we know, they may still do it.

As semen was thought to give off a magical power, it was often used as an offering to the gods in return for favors. When away on long hunting expeditions, prehistoric men gained sexual relief through masturbation, and often had sexual relations with other members of the hunting party. "Terrible!" exclaimed our Victorian ancestors. "They must have been homosexuals." One must remember that such technical terms had not yet been invented, and that people were not yet labelled in groups, as is the modern custom. Most early people were bisexual, and it harmed no one if he gratified himself with members of both sexes, or chose whichever sex he preferred. If people today would only return to this way of thinking, life would be far happier for most. I can remember the horrible fear we had, when I was young, of both masturbation and copulation. It was drilled into us by our parents that if we touched our "private parts" we would become imbeciles, and that if we put our penises near a female, we would catch syphilis and rot away. My own mother, who came from a puritanical family, had her own special tale of horror to scare my brother and myself against sex. She told us that inside a woman's vagina was a set of teeth which would bite off the penis. This prevented us from even talking to girls for several years. We finally believed that if we even shook the hand of a female, we would get some venereal disease. Modern readers may laugh at this, but it certainly frightened my brother and myself and kept us, for a long time, on the straight and narrow path—and this was just over fifty years ago.

When it was finally realized that women had some magic power in their bodies that could convert the male seed into a human being, the female sex organ became an object of worship; not for itself, but as a symbol of the Mother Goddess of Fertility. I have already stated that early man respected anything that vaguely resembled a woman's sexual organ, and how stone circles represented the womb of the Great Mother. Britain is full of these ancient circles, and each one has a phallic stone erected a short distance from it. These are often called King Stones, but the one at Stonehenge is known as the Hele Stone. On Midsummer's Day, crowds still visit the site to see the sun rise over the Hele Stone, but those in the know watch for the shadow of the stone to get longer and longer until it enters the horseshoe shape of Stonehenge itself—a natural symbol of the sex act.

A most remarkable example of sex symbolism left in Britain by the Neolithic people is the famous Men-a-tol, which stands in the heather half a mile from Lanyon Farm, on the Morvah Road, about three miles from Penzance, in Cornwall. This ancient monument consists of three stones—IOI—That is, there are two upright pillars with a huge circle in the middle. The symbolism is obvious, but what is most remarkable is that primitive people, with only stone axes, should have hewn and shaped the mighty O, which is so large that a man can crawl through it. It was once the custom to draw barren women through the hole to cause them to become fertile. Sick children were also passed through it, but now visitors usually scrambled through the o, hoping that it will bring them luck.

Many people have believed that the sexual act is a part of witchcraft rites, but this is entirely wrong. Ordinary copulation could not be used for working magic; if this was the case, couples all over the world would be working magic twenty-four hours a day.

Prehistoric people knew that there was magic that enabled them to reproduce their own kind, and believed it could be produced by a woman's sexual organs and from the male's semen. Druids used the mistletoe in their rites because the berries resembled testicles, and the juice produced when the berries were squeezed was very similar to semen. Since both sexes have orgasms, the climax was considered to be the exact time that the magical power was given off; thus, it was thought that an orgasm could be used to work other magic besides that of creating a baby. This idea led to the belief that masturbation was the answer, and to its introduction into some of the ancient rites. Since semen was being offered to the gods instead of being put into a woman's body, there was one child that would not be born. When the Church turned against the followers of the Old Religion, it used this part of the ancient rite as propaganda against the witches; it was the Christian belief that semen should not be spilled unless to beget children, the Church spread the rumor that the worshipers of the Old Religion sacrificed babies in their ceremonies and, to the church's way of thinking, this was correct. Outsiders, knowing nothing of the old rites, took the Church's words literally, and so we got horrific stories of witches stealing babies in order to sacrifice them to the Devil, or to melt down their fat in order to make flying ointment. These stories suited the Church because they caused many parents to have their children baptized as soon as possible in order to prevent witches from doing this.

As masturbation was used to gain power for magic, it was often found that some women were unable to have a climax solely by manipulating the clitoris, and that some sort of male organ was necessary. This led to the use of the imitation phallus, which we hear so much about in the witch trials. It was the sacred pallus of the God, and the use of it was the same as copulating with the God himself. This idea has been used in many of the ancient religions, and in Egypt, ithyphallic statues of gods, like Min and Osiris, often had a phallus that could be taken off and used for such rites. It has been said that Sappho, of Lesbos, was the high priestess of a witch cult because in one of her poems she mentions a false phallus made of leather. This could be right since she was happily married, and her homosexual relations with her female followers could have been part of some ancient magical rites.

Mating of the two sexes was never part of the old Sabbats, and women seldom returned from these festivals pregnant. Right up to the time of the witch hunts, no woman wanted extra babies, because of the difficulty of obtaining food for those they already had. An extra mouth would not have been welcomed even though the child was fathered by the Devil himself.

Since contraceptives had not yet been invented, women left ordinary copulation alone.

Families which were serfs to the barons and other landowners often stopped their sons from getting married since the son would have to go and work for his wife's employer—this would bring in less food for the family, so that mothers often lay with their own sons when the young men had a sexual urge. If a child was born from such a union, it was considered to be a witch or a magician, because the seed was replanted back in the furrow from whence it came, and the offspring produced was regarded to be gifted with magic powers.

We are told that when a wax figure was used for sympathetic magic, the figure was baptized in holy water in the name of the person who was to be destroyed. This, of course, is a Christianized version, but to a pagan, baptism would not mean anything; besides, image magic was used long before Christianity came into existence. The original figure was made of clay, and given life by mixing it with semen. When the figure was modelled, it was pushed into the sorceress's vagina and kept there for a period that represented the nine months required for the seed to develop. (It is impossible to estimate time periods of the ancients before the days of clocks and such instruments.) It was then removed and cast into a running stream so that it would slowly disintegrate. This was supposed to cause the victim to slowly pine away. All the time the figure was being made, the maker had to concentrate upon the intended victim. The orgasm caused while releasing the semen gave power to the magic.

Sticking pins into wax images came much later, but was not so effective as letting nature destroy it in her own way. Perhaps that is why the witches of North Berwick failed to kill James VI of Scotland by making a wax figure of him. Wax may be easier to model than clay, but it takes away from the idea that we are supposed to be made from clay and will return to clay after death. A clay figure would symbolize this, but a wax one would not. Sympathetic magic must follow nature as nearly as possible. I can understand the idea of using an animal's heart in a love charm, but I cannot see how burning dragon's blood, which is used as a stain by French polishers, can do anything toward softening a person's heart toward someone else.

All charms must contain part of the person for whom they are made, and the old witch, making a love charm for a male, would ask for some semen to add to it. If the client was female, she had to supply some pubic or underarm hair. All of this was accepted by the people of ancient times, but I cannot see this being done in modern times. Perhaps that is why our modern charms don't work. The mass-produced charm or talisman is a complete waste of effort; it contains nothing of the person, and is not even made especially for him. A stone with a hole through it, picked up from the beach is much more effective. At least it is the only one in existence, as no two pebbles are alike, and the finding of it could be looked upon as a gift from the gods.

Women play very important roles in voodoo, and voodoo high priestesses and witch-women frequently force other females to engage in homosexual acts with them. Cunnilingus is often exacted as part payment for magical charms, potions, incantations or prophecies which the native females seek to buy from the mambos.

Madam Tutu, one of the best known and widely feared voodoo practitioners of Port-au-Prince, in Haiti, claimed she kept careful count of the girls and women she had induced to engage in cunnilingus with her over a seventeen-year period: "I've made 6528 of them do it," she boasted, "and I wrote down the names of every one of them—in case I need them."

It is believed that a woman who has performed a homosexual act with a voodoo priestess is thenceforth and forever in the mambo's power, and she must come whenever she is called and do everything she is ordered to do.

It is obvious that followers of voodoo also believe that an orgasm generates a magical power that will aid the charm, incantation, or whatever, but in the case of Madam Tutu, I suggest that as she kept a list of names, she also used this so she could blackmail her clients. One must note that she did not perform the act on her clients, but made them do it to her, and this really gave her power over the women. They could not have told people that the mambo had interfered with them, as they must have willingly performed the act with her. Blackmail often appears in voodoo, and Marie Laveau, who was queen of the New Orleans voodoo, about 1885, was not against using blackmail to obtain money. Many of her young women followers worked as personal maids to wealthy people, and this enabled Marie to get to know the latest scandal and use it to her own avantage.

The witches pole dance, which they used to make crops grow by hobbyhorsing around the field on a pole, was also sex magic. Originally a pole was used, often carved to represent a phallus; but during the witch-hunts they used a broom because the pole might lead to a conviction. The real witches' broom was made of heather tied to a stick; hence its name.

The dance was done by holding the broom with the pole between the legs, so that the lower end came in contact with the clitoris; while the witch danced, she moved the broom up and down so that the action caused her to have an orgasm. In later years, the dance seemed to change, and instead of obtaining the power by sex magic, witches depended on the speed of the dance, which got faster and faster until they all dropped with exhaustion, something like the method used by the dancing dervishers.

One must remember that the behavior of people in the Middle Ages was extremely bawdy, and four-letter words were common in ordinary conversation. When James VI of Scotland became king of England, he could not understand why the English people liked to see their king, and when told that they only wanted to see his face, he shouted, "God's wounds! I'll pull down my breeches and they shall see my arse!" The expression "riding a broom" did not mean flying through the air on a broomstick; it meant having unnatural inter-course with a broom handle. The word *ride* for the sex act is recorded before 1250, and was general English until about 1780. "Broom" and "brush" were also vulgar expressions for a woman's pubic hair, so that the "broom between her legs" had quite a different meaning from what it would mean today.

Sex magic also appears to be part of spiritualism, and to quote from the book *Between Two Worlds*: "In 1934, Mrs. Bullock, a medium, said that during the transfiguration process she had the positive sensation of a hand massaging her womb. This had lent support to a finding that has been publicized in parapsychological research, that the medium draws on her sexual energies for the production of such phenomena, that she acts as if she actually were to give birth to the phantoms that led researchers on such a heartbreaking chase."

N'Bdo women practice lycanthropy and believe that they can change themselves into leopards. They keep tame female leopards in the village compound as pets, and twice a year, at periods that correspond to the summer and winter solstice, they hold weekend ceremonies. During these periods, they assume the characteristics of leopards, and according to their belief, the spirits of the leopards enter their bodies. Mass marathon homosexual excesses are part of these rites.

This is similar to an old European witch rite held to produce fertility in cattle. The witches, wearing masks of the particular animals, fasten on a false phallus, and have intercourse with another woman in the animal position. This is pure sympathetic magic.

Cured or mummified sexual organs of various animals are used in cult rituals of several central African tribes. Among the Mwakamani of the eastern Cameroons, the climax of several magical rituals calls for two or more women to mount a platform, which is an architectural adjunct of all native villages, and there simulate coitus using these phalli. These women also engage in mass homosexual practices during which the males of the tribe must remain hidden in their huts. Any man who sees any part of these magical rituals is killed by the witch-woman of the village. There are usually two or three of these witches to every village. They are required to be homosexual. Unlike other women of the tribe, they may not engage in heterosexual relations with the men under any circumstances, and must not bear children. If they fail to observe either of these taboos, they are instantly killed. The witches act as mistresses of ceremonies for the homosexual magical rites, and determine the acts to be performed by the various women in addition to participation in the rites themselves.

The witches of ancient Britain led lives similar to these central African witch-women, and until fairly recent times the majority of witches in Britain were unmarried, but they usually had a younger woman as a companion. Many of the old pictures of witches show this. In one way, all females are bisexual, because they possess a clitoris, the rudimentary organ analogous to the male penis. A technical term is *penis mulicbrus* and a popular expression for it is the "man in the boat"; the boat being the oval shape of the female organ. The oval is also a symbolic sign of the Great Mother.

The crescent moon also symbolizes the female organ, and was often depicted as a boat, sometimes with a man in it, as in a picture from Ur, dated between 2300 and 2100 B.C. It is now in the British Museum. An Assyrian winged moon, from a cylinder of about the eighteenth dynasty, also shows a man in a crescent moon. Streams of heavenly nectar pour down from it, and is caught in two goblets. This is the female fluid obtained by masturbation, and was considered to contain magic of great power.

The sign of the sacred moon tree, from an ancient Italian carving found in the Barberini Palace in Rome, and pre-Christian carvings found in Greek churches also symbolize the clitoris—the female penis. The Babylonian moon god, Sinn, too, symbolizes the clitoris, and for this reason, Christian priests, who were very antifemale, used his name to denote their idea of sin. He is also shown in a crescent moon. The common expression "man in the boat" for the clitoris is a folk memory of this ancient symbol. The high priest, standing in his position at the top end of the witches' circle also represents the female organ.

Homosexual rites, as well, took place in the magician's circle. The late Aleister Crowley used several of them, but these have already been written up by other authors. The boy, or young man, assistant to the magician was used to obtain semen for use in the magical rites, and this action has been translated into sacrifices of young boys by the enemies of the old magicians. Homosexual rites also brought out the female side of the magician. This was originally done so that he could represent the gods, who were mostly bisexual.

4

The Goat and the Witch

Why was the goat always associated with Witches? Many people think it is because this animal represents the God Pan—who in turn depicted the animal nature in man—and because of its powers of fertility. This seems to suggest that all witches were nymphomaniacs and only attended the Sabbat to be raped by the Horned God or someone representing him. This was not so.

The Horned God of the Witches was a god of hunting and death, and not a god of fertility like Pan. People of the Stone Age could never have heard of Pan, nor of any other foreign gods, and kept to their own deities.

Many writers have written about the history of the witches' god, and of how he was born from the ancient method of hunting: a man dressed in the skin of an animal, and wearing a pair of antlers on his head, would rush among the beasts, causing them to stampede over the cliffs. Since many of these hunters must have been crushed by the cattle, the God also represented death, and those who died were looked upon as sacrifices to the God.

This deity was not a god of fertility; he came into being before man learned that the male was responsible for impregnating women and while man still believed that the female produced babies entirely by herself.

One can learn more truth by the study of folklore than by reading books on history, which are always biased by the ideas of the writers. Take one example from English history. Richard I was never known as Coeur-de-Lion (the Lion-hearted) in his lifetime, but as Richard Oc-e-No, Richard Yes-and-No. He was not the great national hero that history has made him, but rather had much in common with the gangsters of old Chicago—always fighting, feuding, killing and betraying to obtain more territory. As for his being a popular English king, Richard considered his French possessions more important than his English ones, and in his ten-years reign spent only about six months in England, and did not even bother to learn the language of his own people. His role of crusader enabled him to get away from routine and the worries of governing his people. The nearest he ever came to Jerusalem was a view of it from a nearby hill. Quarrels among the crusaders themselves caused the Crusade to be a complete failure, and the only thing that these supposed heroes brought back to Europe was syphilis.

Historians gloss over the dark side of their heroes,

and omit anything they don't agree with. In England, schoolchildren are only taught English history from the time of the Roman invasion, and therefore believe that the earliest Britons were nothing but painted savages. All culture previous to the invasion has been ignored.

Although the dictionary states that "history is the narration of facts," many great thinkers have other ideas about it. Napoleon said, "history is a fable agreed upon"; Nietzsche declared, "history is nothing more than the belief in falsehood," and the well-known writer H. G. Wells referred to that "poison called history." Delve into the folklore and legends of any country, and much truth can be read between the lines.

Legends of the demon hunter, which can be found all over Europe, prove the existence of a horned god. The town of Windsor has one such legend: Herne the Hunter haunts the park that belongs to Windsor Castle. Herne is said to be dressed in skins and to wear a pair of antlers on his head. He is also said to appear on the battlements of the castle at the death of the monarch. Obviously, Herne is the old god of hunting and death.

Alderly Edge, that bleak and wild spot in Cheshire, also has its horned hunter, and a wild hunt called the Herlathing. It is said that a wizard guards King Arthur and his knights, who lie sleeping in a hollow hill, ready to rise and fight again when the magic stone that binds them is found. Other places in Britain have this legend of the sleeping knights, including Richmond, in Yorkshire, where King Arthur and the knights lie asleep in some secret room under the castle.

Arthur was one of the English names for the old god, and these legends prove that the old religion went underground, and that its followers believed it would return.

In Lincoln Cathedral is a carving of a horned figure, now called the "Lincoln Imp." Obviously, the old god was put there by a stonemason who must have followed the old religion and when the church was built on the ancient sacred site, the stonemason carved him among various Christian symbols so that he would not be forgotten. The carving is in a prominent position, on one of the columns, so that the early Christians and the worshipers of the old gods must have worked side by side. The old carver did his work well, and the Lincoln Imp is as famous as the Cathedral itself; models of the horned figure in brass are sold by the thousands to visitors. Since the revival of witchcraft, and because several writers have explained that the famous emblem of Lincoln represents the old god, those connected with the Cathedral have tried to make another carving, the Pilgrim, the souvenir of Lincoln. They are having very little success, as the Horned God has ruled over Lincolnshire far too long to be easily brushed aside.

All names like Herne, Alan, Robin, Arthur, Hornie and Nick, among others, were localized names for the old god, and places that have legends connected with such names, or villages or towns that are known by these names or have them incorporated in their names, were the meeting places of the old covens. Such places usually have a grove, hill or well that was once sacred to the old deities.

One of the Yorkshire names for the Horned God was Hob. Hob still haunts parts of the Yorkshire Moors, where there are remains of ancient stone circles. Runwick Bay, near Whitby, has a cave called

Hob's Hole, and until recently country women whose children suffered with whooping cough took them to the cave and called out: "Hob-hole Hob! Ma bairn's gotten t'king-cough. Tak't off—Tak't off!" Unfortunately, Hob has lost his old godly attributes, and is now looked upon as a mischievous hobgoblin.

To return to the subject of the goat and Witches, one must remember that the goat and the dog were the first wild animals to be domesticated. Man chose the dog because it would help him with his hunting. Folk memory proves this by giving us the saying, "man's best friend is his dog."

The goat had more of a domesticated use, and stayed at home with the woman. It was a most useful creature. It gave milk, from which cheese could be made; its flesh could be eaten, and its skin used for making clothes and shoes; while its horns could be used to make domestic and agricultural implements, such as picks, spoons, and drinking vessels. The goat could also be used as a beast of burden, and after the invention of the wheel it was used to pull small carts. The animal was easy to keep, since it would eat almost anything, and because it bred easily, it became a symbol of fertility. As the females of the clans tended and milked it, the goat became associated with women. In the Middle Ages and even later, the old witches, who very often lived alone, nearly always kept a goat.

Another reason why the goat was associated with witches is a symbolic one. Early man, having no written language, visualized all things as pictures. He had an imagination that was far more vivid than that of most people today. This is proved by the fantastic figures he saw in the night sky. What early man visualized in the stars has come down to us in the names of the various constellations: the Great Bear, the Goat, the Lion, Orion, and so on. How many people can see these figures by just looking at the heavens? We recognize these groups of stars only because we have been told what they are supposed to be, and because we keep the same figures that the ancients saw centuries ago. Prehistoric cave drawings show that early man viewed everything through the eyes of an artist. He was an expert at seeing pictures in the fire, or in anything else.

Early man, while watching witches work in the nude, saw the figure of a goat's head in the lower part of their bodies—the pubic triangle, with its hair. This, with a little imagination, is a perfect representation of a goat's head (see illustration).

Also, a woman standing with her legs apart and her arms outstretched in the pentacle position, as it is known in the craft, forms a goat's head with her torso, arms and breasts (see illustration).

With these aspects in mind, it can be seen clearly why the witch was associated with the goat, and how this animal became "part" of the female. From our first example, one can easily understand why some of the early peoples described a witch as having a goat between her legs; this notion later gave birth to pictures of witches riding goats to the Sabbats.

As I have already mentioned in Chapter 3, the expression "to ride" was used to describe having sexual intercourse. The idea of a witch riding a goat was easily changed, for propaganda purposes, into stories that witches had sexual relations with goats. This caused the Satanists—those seventeenth-century cults of devil-worshipers which seemed to use a lot of

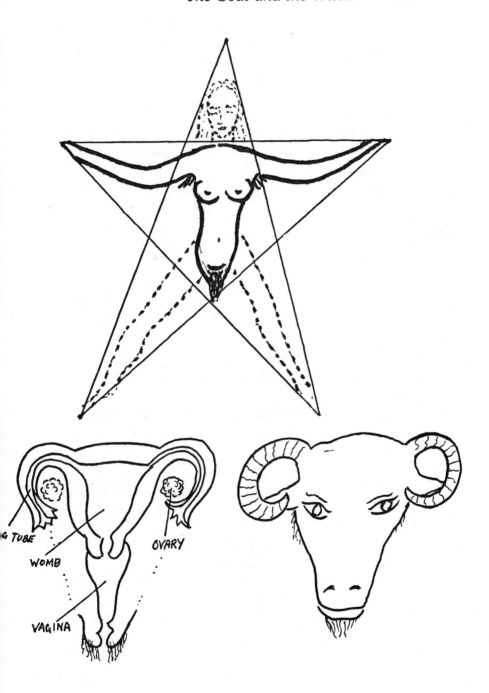

TUBE

WOMB

OVARY

VAGINA

senseless mumbo-jumbo, such as saying prayers backward, and reversing church rituals in black masses—to introduce a satanic rite in which a woman was raped by a goat.

This ritual rape was not a magic rite; nothing could be achieved by it except gratification of a morbid depravity in the aged and aristocratic playboys of the time of Sir Francis Dashwood's Hellfire Club in the caves at High Wycombe.

Although this act of beastiality was said to be a part of black magic, I very much doubt that it ever was. It is also doubtful that a goat would willingly copulate with a human being. Such a match was actually tried out in the time of the caesars at the coliseum, in hopes that the spectacle would attract more people than fighting gladiators or Christians thrown to lions; but the different animals they hoped would rape the women were not interested. One famous animal trainer suggested that the women be dressed in the skins of the particular beasts that were supposed to perform the rape. This would impregnate the skin of the women with the animals' scent. Even so, the experiment was not too successful, and the exhibition was dropped for more blood-thirsty spectacles.

The female body has given us other witchcraft symbols, such as the triangle, the broom and the goose foot. The illustrations will show how they came about. The complete broom symbolized the sex act; the handle being the phallus, and the sweeping end the female organ. It has also been suggested that the symbol of the ram's head portrays the internal sexual organs of the female. The illustration shows how these

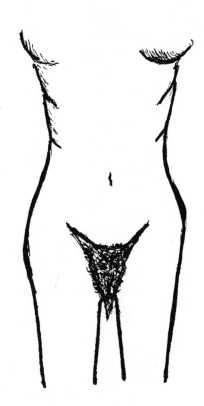

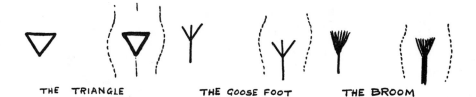

THE TRIANGLE   THE GOOSE FOOT   THE BROOM

organs bear a resemblance to the head of the ram (see illustration).

The representation of the Goddess of the Witches by a goat's head was originated so that she could not be identified with any living woman; otherwise, every artist would have his own idea of what the Goddess should look like, and would insert the features of the woman he liked best.

NOTE: In *The White Goddess*, poet and author Robert Graves has written: "The god of the witches is held by Dr. [Margaret] Murray to be a lineal descendant of a paleolithic goat or stag god who later became the Gaullish Cernunnus, and Shakespeare's Herne the Hunter. Yet the lighted candle which every grand master, disguised as a black he-goat, wore between his horns on the great witches Sabbath—whether in England or in France—points in a very different direction. Idries Shah Sayed, the Sufi historian, has shown that a candle set between two horns emblemised the ninth-century Aniza school of mystics, founded by Abu-el-Ataahia. Abu came from the powerful Arabian Aniza [Goat] tribe, to which our contemporaries, Ibn Saud's sons and the Ruler of Kuwait belong. The candle therefore meant 'illumination from the head of Aniza.' "

Graves' thesis is that this goat-head symbol stems from the Aniza school and also the Berber Cult of the Two-Horned God. Other authorities dispute this, saying that the goat- and stag-horn symbolisms are indigenous to the countries where found. What he says about the Aniza and Berber sects is true enough, but their influence on European witchcraft is historically moot, although there is much evidence of contact between them.

For more on the symbolism and ancient heritage of horns see the chapter "Holy Horns and Halos" in Dr. Martello's book *Witchcraft: The Old Religion*.

L.L.M.

5

Halloween

Halloween was the end of the year, the time when the Goddess returned to the underworld; when Mother Nature took her winter sleep beneath her blanket of snow. There she rested until the vegetation began to grow again. On this night the Horned God began his reign.

In the days when witchcraft was purely a woman's cult, the high priestess represented the Goddess during the summer months, and at the Halloween ritual she placed a horned helmut upon her head and fastened on a false phallus in order to play the role of the God. She continued to do this until it was time for the Goddess to take over again.

Later, when men infiltrated the craft, the high priest played the part of the Horned One. In modern covens, where there are no male members, a female still takes the part of the God, but, due to our puritanical upbringing, a sword replaces the phallus. The phallus was originally made of leather, and attached to a belt.

The ancient rite took place in one of the old stone circles, and was always performed in the nude. Some of the witches wore cloaks when going to the meeting place, but others just traveled naked. Nobody took note of this, as people were accustomed to seeing nude folk going to the Sabbats.

The circle did not need to be magically drawn as in modern ritual, since the standing-stones formed a permanent sacred circle which was not used for any other purpose. It was a temple to the old gods, and, like a modern church, did not have to be consecrated with every use. Since no one went to these sites except to worship, they were not overrun by sightseers as they are today. They were held in great reverence by the followers of the old faith, and even the early Christians respected them until the Church became strong enough to try and destroy the ancient gods. Later, vandals damaged many of the sites, or, as at Avebury, masons broke up many of the stones for building purposes. Avebury is among the largest stone circles in Britain; it now has a village inside it.

When the worshipers arrived at the venue, they took their places around the circle and stood with their arms raised and their fingers and thumbs touching, the thumbs stretched as far as possible. This formed a kind of oval, representing the female sexual organ—a symbol of the Great Mother.

The assistant to the high priestess, usually called the "maiden," made her appearance. She was completely naked, except for a necklace of small stones, each one having a natural hole through it. In her right hand she carried a horn. Walking in a stately manner to each of the four points of the compass, she raised the horn to her lips and blew a long blast. This was to summon the minor gods, whom modern Witches refer to as the Lords of the Outer Spaces.

Putting the horn aside, the maiden moved over to the center of the circle and faced north, and falling upon her knees, bowed low; the rest of the witches copied her actions. This signalled the high priestess to make her appearance. A complete hush fell over the assembly, interrupted only by the cries of night birds and the occasional hooting of an owl in a nearby tree. With solemn tread, the priestess made her appearance between the two standing-stones at the northern edge of the circle. She wore a long white robe and a rowan crown on her head. In later years, a silver crown was used, ornamented with a crescent moon; silver being the sacred metal of the Goddess.

After chanting a prayer, the maiden called on the spirit of the Goddess to descend upon the high priestess. Unfortunately, in most cases the words of such prayers have been lost in time (only a very few have come down to us), but we can assume that it was a prayer of thanks for a good harvest and for blessings that the Goddess bestowed upon the people during the summer months.

After this, the priestess held her arms aloft and let the cloak fall from her shoulders, exposing her naked body to full view of the worshipers. This was done so that she could give out the full power from her body, without any of it being absorbed by the garment. With this sign that the spirit of the Great Mother had

entered the body of the high priestess, all of the
worshipers called out, in unison, "Hail to thee Great
Goddess."

Then the maiden handed the high priestess a
lighted torch, with which she kindled the bonfire which
had already been piled up in the center of the circle.
When the fire began to blaze, a number of the worshipers came forward with bundles of wheat and oats, and
baskets of fruit and vegetables, casting them into the
flames as a sacrifice to the Goddess. Vessels of beer
and cider were poured on the ground, all around the
circle, as a libation. This ceremony was adopted by the
Christians in their harvest festivals, but the original
meaning is lost because goods are no longer sacrificed
to the gods.

After the offerings had been made, the witches
began their round dance. They held hands and pranced
around the blazing fire. The pace got faster and faster
until they fell to the ground in exhaustion.

This was the last dance of the year in honor of the
Goddess, as she was soon to leave the world of men.
There was a sadness among the company. Saying
"Farewell" to the Great Mother was like parting with
an old friend, and all the witches covered their faces
with their hands as a sign of sadness.

The high priestess, in her role of Goddess, bade the
witches farewell, promising to return again when the
trees were green. Then the company raised their right
hands as a parting sign. The maiden replaced the cloak
on the priestess's shoulders and followed her out of the
circle.

The two women then set off toward the King
Stone—the phallic symbol of the God. The high priestess kissed the stone and, turning around, stood with

her back and the palms of her hands pressed against the stone. She remained in this position for a long time, absorbing into her body the male power of the God. Then, she nodded her head, giving the signal for the maiden to remove the crown and replace it with a horned helmet. The priestess crossed her hands over her breasts, and the maiden fastened onto her the imitation phallus. The priestess had now been symbolically and mentally transformed into the God, and would appear this way at all Sabbats and esbats during the winter months. Once more, she dropped the cloak, and was handed a forked ash rod, another symbol of the Horned God, and returned to the circle. There she was hailed as the Horned God of Hunting and Death. This sex-changing ritual accounted for the many pictures and statues of bisexual gods; it was not, as many people think, because the gods were hermaphrodites. The priestess could add a male penis to her body, but since she could not lose her female breasts, the image of the god became bisexual and did not become wholly male until men entered the craft and became high priests.

Halloween has always been the Festival of the Dead, and was believed to be the best time to contact those who had passed over. Today, spiritualists try to contact the departed by means of "spirit guides"— American Indians, Chinese men, nuns, priests and even little girls. Witches tried to make contact through the God of Death himself. So when the bonfire had burned down, and an eerie atmosphere was created by the great stones that stood out like specters in the darkness, the priestess, in her new role as the God, held a skull between her hands, using it as a crystal-gazing ball. This was the kind of necromancy practiced centuries before the Fox Sisters, with their poltergeist tappings, started the modern craze for spiritualism.

Some of the Celts used to lie on graves, hoping to receive a message from the person who lay beneath. This was long before Christian churchyards were established, but the knowledge of this ancient custom gave rise to stories of witches performing diabolical rites in graveyards. The high priestesses were just as successful in contacting the dead as are our own mediums; when this part of the ceremony was concluded, the gods were evoked and the meeting came to an end. Then the feast began: the worshipers brought out the food and drink that they had brought with them, sharing among all who were present. The feast was the social side of the craft. As most of the participants saw each other only at the Sabbats, they would chat and laugh among themselves, relating the latest news and scandal from the various villages. This would carry on until the cock crowed, then they would all go off in different directions.

After the craft had become a mixed cult, this feast would have been the time when any sexual intercourse took place; but intercourse was not a general practice nor an orgiastic part of the rites. The festival was no different then any held today. One must not judge all the people of a group by the way a few of them behave. The same could happen if boy meets girl after a church service. It was the persecutors of the witches who seized upon any sexual lapses and enlarged upon them, solely to blacken the image of the craft.

England has dropped its Halloween festivities, no doubt because Guy Fawkes Day, with its bonfires, happens to fall on November 5, the thought being that two fire festivals so close together would cancel each other out. The Scottish still celebrate Halloween with parties, and special cakes, with pictures of witches on them, can be bought in their shops. It still remains a time of prophecy, and numerous methods of foretelling the future, especially ways of discovering who one will wed, have come down to us. These folk customs have been preserved for future generations in the writings of Robert Burns, Scotland's national bard. If Burns himself was not a Witch, he certainly knew a lot about the witchlore of his times, as his poems show.

6

The Lone Witch

I have often been asked if a
person can follow the old
religion without being initi-
ated into a coven. There are many people who live in
country districts, or are far away from places where
covens exist, and yet they desire to worship the old
gods. I see no reason why they should not do this,
providing they are sincere and believe in the God and
Goddess.

Some modern witches enjoy the theatrical side of
ritual, and enjoy dressing up in robes, using swords
and other showy equipment; their altars look like an
antiques stall in a market. All this is unnecessary; none
of the ancient witches had this pomp and paraphernalia. Aleister Crowley said of the magician, that unless
he was sincere and knew the right way to use the
various props, they were of no more value than the

70

junk from a rag-and-bone man's wheelbarrow.* When I met Crowley, toward the end of his life, he had given up all of his magical props; he said that he could achieve the same results with a candle on his bedside table, a cone of incense, and his penknife in place of a magic sword. It was the magician, himself, who mattered; not the tools of the trade. Fanciful instruments and other paraphernalia was purely part of the showmanship used to impress outsiders.

During the days of witch-hunts, no witch dared to use ritual items for fear of being convicted. Witches converted any domestic article that was suitable—a table knife, with the magical signs chalked on the handle, a chalk-drawn circle and any old vessels that would hold liquids. The caldron, itself, was a domestic article in those days. The circle and other chalk-drawn signs could be rubbed out. It was like the French Underground Movement during World War II, when radio transmitters, weapons and other instruments had to be disguised and easily hidden at a moment's notice.

Very few tools are necessary for the lone worker, and anyone can easily make his own. Any knife can be used as an athame, and although it is customary to have a knife with a black handle, this is not a necessity, but one should use the same knife every time and keep it for ritual purposes only. It is best to carry the knife on one's person, as it absorbs a certain amount of power from the owner's body. The late Gerald Gardner used an old hunting knife, which he always carried with him in a sheath attached to his belt. He used it whenever he wanted to cut anything,

* Our "rag" or "junkman."

and we often saw him using it as a table knife when no other was available.

The signs on the athame are emblems, or symbols, of the craft, like the symbols on Masonic swords, but are not necessary for carrying out rituals. If one wishes to have the signs, they can be found in several books on witchcraft; but since they appear to differ so much, it is perhaps just as well to omit them.

A white-handled knife was once used for making things in the circle, but as most props can be bought today, it is now seldom used.

The only cord necessary for the lone witch is one just over four-and-a-half-feet long. By fastening one end to the ground with a nail or a drawing pin, and winding the other end around a piece of chalk, it is easy to draw a nine-foot circle. Nine is the number of the Moon and, as the circle represents the womb of the Great Mother, it also represents the number of months it takes for the embryo to grow into a human being. When working in the open, the chalk can be replaced by a penknife, or a piece of stick, and a circle cut into the ground.

A sword is unnecessary; no ancient witch ever possessed one. Instead, she used a length of hazel-wood, about eighteen inches long, cut from the tree with her athame. This is the simplest way to make a magic wand, and the hazelwood has the same effect as the sword.

Some covens use pictures or statues of the God and Goddess. These are only reminders of the deities, in the same way that Catholics use statues of the Sacred Heart, the Virgin Mary, or various saints. For this purpose, the old witch used a stang, that is, a forked hazel rod. One with two prongs represented the

Horned God, and one with three prongs was used for the Goddess. Sometimes a pitchfork was used as an emblem for the God.

When performing a ritual to the God, the two-fork stang was stuck in the ground; the three-pronged stang was used when the rite was for the Goddess. When working indoors, one must make a stand for the stangs; a block of wood with two holes will do.

One will also require three small bowls, or other vessels, for holding salt and water, and for burning the sacrifice. For the latter purpose, one can use a scallop shell, which is symbolic of the Goddess; legend tells us that, as Venus, she rose from the sea in such a shell.

The pentacle is a brass plate on which is engraved the symbols of the craft: a down-pointed triangle; a reversed pentacle, or star; an upright pentacle, crowned by a triangle; a circle with a crescent on top, symbolizing the full and crescent Moon, and also the Horned God; two *S*'s crossed with a downward line; and two crescent moons back to back. These symbols can be painted on a round flat stone. The stone is a more recent addition to witch rites, and may have been suggested by the pentacles and talismans used by magicians in ritual magic. Statues of the deities, for the altar, can be replaced by a stone with a natural hole through it, to represent the Goddess, and a phallic-shaped pebble, to symbolize the God. These can be easily picked up on stoney beaches.

The altar can be a small table or, for working outside, a flat piece of rock or a large stone may be employed.

Five candles are required: one on the altar, and one at each point of the compass. If candlesticks cannot be obtained, empty bottles may be used. When working alfresco, one can prevent the candles from being blown out by using candle lanterns that can be purchased cheaply from shops that supply camping equipment.

When performing the rites indoors, one should be completely naked. Female witches should wear a necklace, as this, being a circle, is another symbol of the Goddess. Those made from natural materials— such as stones with holes in them, nuts, acorns, or even a chain of daisies—are best. One braided from human hair is believed to be most powerful. When outdoors, in places like England, where the summer usually consists of only a few days of fine weather, one usually wears as much as possible, covered by a hooded cloak. It is not advisable to perform winter rites out of doors unless one has the constitution of a mountain goat.

Before entering the circle, one should take a bath, adding natural herbs to the water if desired. Bath salts, deodorizers, perfumes and makeup should be left alone. One should enter the circle as one came out of the womb, and no one was born with lipstick, rouge or false eyelashes. Females should let their hair flow naturally, free from hairpins, hair bands and other contrivances. Men should refrain from talcum powder and aftershave lotion.

If one is working in a room with a carpet, or for some other reason a circle cannot be drawn with chalk, one can make a nine-foot circle out of a piece of string or rope. No true witch would ever make a circle of plastic or some other synthetic material. One must get as near to nature as possible. Even electric fires can interfere with the working of the magic, so oil heating is best.

The circle and all the tools to be used should be readied before one bathes, so that afterward one can immediately enter the circle, for once inside, the circle should not be broken until the rites are completed.

CASTING THE CIRCLE

Although the circle is marked upon the ground, it must be drawn with the magic knife or wand. First, light the candle on the altar, then the four that are at the edge of the circle, in the north, west, south and east. When this has been done, take the knife, or wand, and hold it above the candle in the west. Then, slowly move the wand through the air and around the circle, and continue until you arrive back at your starting point. This must be done with all seriousness, and at the same time try to visualize that you are drawing a circle of fire. Say: "O thou circle, be thou a protection against all evil powers and spirits, so that those within will be kept free and pure from all outside influences."

Now light the incense. If joss sticks are used, a small bowl of sand will be found useful to hold them. They can even be stuck in half a potato, which will act as a stand. Carry the incense around the circle, starting from the west, saying: "I scent thee, O circle, so that this sweet-smelling perfume will only attract good spirits and drive away all evil influences." Return the incense to the altar and, taking up the salt, sprinkle it into the bowl of water, saying: "I mix this creature of salt with this creature of water, and when combined it becomes a purifying fluid which is sacred to the God and Goddess. I do this in the name of Hob and Anu." (Because each locality had its own names for the deities, I am using the accepted names from East Riding, in Yorkshire, which was the home of the Briganti tribe in the Celtic period.)

Take the holy water and sprinkle it all around the circle, saying: "I purify this circle in the names of Hob and Anu." Stand by the altar, which should be in the north, and sprinkle yourself with the water, saying: "I purify myself with this water so that I may be in a fit state to serve the gods of our ancient craft." You then scent yourself with the incense. This is done by making the sign of the triangle, as near to the body as possible, with the bowl of incense held in both hands. If a male, an upright triangle is formed; if female, a triangle is formed with its apex pointed downward. Then say: "I now offer myself as a sacrifice to the gods, and ask you to accept this gift of bodily power from your servant and priest (or priestess).

When this is said, some hair from the pubes and underarms is cut off with the athame and burned in the shell. (Again this is symbolic, as the two armpits and the pubic area form a downward triangle, the sign of the Goddess.)

Now take the wand, and going to the west, point it in that direction. Make the sign of the pentacle in the air, and call out in a loud voice: "I summon, stir and call thee up, ye Mighty Ones of the west to witness the rites and to guard the circle."

Then you proceed to the south and repeat this at the other three points of the compass.

Now stand up the two-pronged stang and, with the wand in your hand, make a "V" sign in the air (the God sign), saying: "I invoke thee O Dreaded One. Be thou present during the rite, and aid me in the arts magical." Gaze intently at the stang until you can visualize the Horned God himself. With practice, providing the invocation is done with sincerity, you will feel the presence of the God with you.

The female stang is then set up, and the Goddess invoked with her sign, the downward triangle: "I invoke thee, O Gentle Goddess and mother of us all, to be present at this rite and to aid me in my magic work."

I have described the invocation of both deities, but usually only one is invoked, that is, the one who rules over that particular time of the year at which the rite is being performed. From Candlemas to Halloween it is the Goddess; the rest of the year it is the God.

PRAYING TO THE DEITIES

In some covens the members kneel when praying, but this has been borrowed from the Christians. The witches always stood in prayer. If a general prayer was being said, they bent their arms at the elbows and turned the palms toward the north, with the fingers stretched upright.

If praying to the God, the fingertips were placed together so that the hands formed the male sign of the upright triangle.

If the prayer was to the Goddess, the fingers were placed together with the tips touching, and the heels of the hands also touching. The thumbs were placed one on top of the other, and the fingers slightly bent. This formed an oval, the shape of the female sexual organ, and the thumbs represented the clitoris.

PRAYER BEFORE WORKING MAGIC

O Gracious Goddess, Queen of Night,
I ask you to accept this rite
And send me all your mystic power
To aid me this important hour.
In castle, cottage, sacred glade;
Where ere the circle shall be made.
I pray that you will grant this boon
O lovely Goddess of the Moon.

The best time to work magic is from the new moon until it is full. Magic rites should not be performed during the waning moon.

HOW TO WORK MAGIC

Witches have never believed that their gods are all powerful, but that these gods need man's help as man needs theirs. It is necessary for gods and men to work together in harmony. That is why these gods are nearer to us than the Christian God is to them. We approach them directly and not through a mediator, as the Catholics do with the Virgin Mary and other saints. Witches also believe that what pleases humans also pleases the gods, that is why wine is poured on the ground as a libation to them. The gods are able to help us obtain our wishes through magic, but they need an earthly power to do this. This power comes from the worshiper's own body.

We have explained in Chapter 3 how offerings of semen and other sex-magic was performed by the old witches, but most modern witches raise this power by the dance. This can be done by a person working alone, but it takes more time to do than when a lot of people are working together. You will never get immediate results. Magic, like all other arts, requires practice. If you do not believe that magic works, then do not attempt it, as in this state of mind it certainly will not. You must think magically; in fact, we might almost say, you must live magic; not believing, but knowing it *will* work.

In one way it is easier for a lone worker to work magic than it is for a full coven. The coven can raise the power quickest, but every single member of the group must concentrate on what is required, as if they were all one mind. This is not easy. When a number of people are working for what one of them wants, there is often someone who doesn't really care if that person gets his wish or not, since it doesn't affect him. Unless every single person is determined that the magic will work, it will fail.

The lone Witch knows what he or she wants, and is determined to get it at all costs. It is the one thought in their mind, and there is no one unconsciously working against it.

Most things that one desires are controlled by somebody else's mind, and it is necessary to change that person's mind in favor of yourself, so that he will give, sell or do something else you want him to do.

Place the knife on the altar so that it is pointing in the direction of the place where that person lives, or is most likely to be at that moment. Then think out a simple rhyme describing what you require. For example, you want a certain person to give you a job. You have applied for it, and it is only necessary to make him pick you from among the other applicants. Make up a simple jingle like this:

> So and so (name) give me the job.
> Help me Anu; help me Hob.

or,

> Mr. (name) pick me out.
> I am the best there is no doubt.

This may sound very childish, but the verse quickly plants the idea in your subconscious mind and allows you to concentrate more easily.

Now, start walking slowly around the circle, repeating the verse, over and over again as you go around. Quicken your speed as you go around until you find yourself running at a great speed, and the circle will appear to be flying around you. Continue until you get giddy, or almost drop with exhaustion. You may have to repeat this several times on different occasions, but finally you will receive a letter to say that the person requires your services. We find that in almost ninety cases out of a hundred this method of magic works.

If you are working for somebody who is ill, you must know exactly what that illness is, or what part of the body is affected. Then work out a jingle to fit the case. It is no use generalizing:

> O lovely Goddess of the Moon
> Make Mary Ellen get well soon.

You must pinpoint the trouble, and also visualize that person while you are going around.

My wife, Patricia, is universally known as a Witch owing to her television appearances, and gets hundreds of letters from people wanting her help. Some people just want her to make them win the football pool or bring them easy money some other way; however, many requests come from people who are ill and really need help. The former she just ignores, but she will always try to help any sick person; yet, it is very difficult to work for people who are unknown to you—you have no one to concentrate upon. Patricia always writes and asks for a photograph of the sick person so that she will have some sort of contact with him, and will have something to concentrate on. It is surprising how many people refuse to send a picture of themselves. Either they fear that their friends may find out that they have sought help from a witch, or they believe that a photograph is part of them and that any witch possessing one has power over them. This belief is common among tribesmen.

After many years as practicing Witches, we have had a great many cures by using a photograph. We find that the best way is to have one of the members of the coven sit in the center of the circle and concentrate upon the picture, while the rest dance around to raise the power.

It is advisable not to try and work more than one cure on the same night. If it is done properly, it will take a great deal of energy, and each work of magic should be started while the Witch is fresh. People who seek a Witch's help do not realize what this method of working takes out of the Witch. It is like giving part of yourself in exchange for a successful result. The outsider imagines it is all achieved by a simple wave of a magic wand. One woman we managed to cure from a very serious illness wrote afterward and sent a long list of other things she wanted us to do for her. I wrote back and told her that even in fairy stories people were only allowed three wishes. We never heard from her again.

When you have completed your magic, you should thank the God and Goddess for their aid—in your own words—and then evoke them. This is done by making their invocation sign in the air, with the wand, in the direction opposite to that by which you invoked them.

This invocation sign is the reversed pentacle. Make it in the air, with the magic wand, and say: "I thank you for attending, and ere you return to your lovely realms, I bid ye hail and farewell."

Some covens finish the evening with what has become known as "cakes and wine." This is just a small snack and drink, for the benefit of those who have travelled to the meeting. The food and drink are blessed in the names of the deities. This is not really part of the rites, and is not necessary for those working alone in their own homes. It is just a memento from the days of the great Sabbats when the ceremony concluded with a huge feast. Everyone brought some kind of food, and often whole sheep were roasted on the fire.

"Drawing Down the Moon" is a rite to cause the spirit of the Goddess to descend upon and enter the body of the high priestess. When it is successfully performed, the priestess will often speak in a strange voice and give out messages that are helpful to the coven or, sometimes, just to an individual person.

Whenever this happens, the priestess goes into a complete trance; when she comes out of it, she has no idea of what she has been saying. This rite cannot be worked by just one witch, and is never done for a male.

In the next chapter, we intend to give you rites for the four main festivals which can be worked by a lone witch. Remember that on all occasions when one is working in the circle, a ritual bath must be taken first, the circle drawn and concentrated, and the worshipper purified. After the rites have been performed, the circle must be closed by evoking the deities and the Lords of the Outer Spaces. As these have already been described, I will not repeat them.

NOTE: Compare what the Crowthers write here with what two other American Gardnerians say about the lone Witch in the chapter "Interview with a Gardnerian Witch High Priestess and High Priest" in Dr. Martello's *Witchcraft: The Old Religion*. The question asked was: "If someone would like to worship the ancient deities, but because of circumstance or geographical distance cannot make contact with a genuine Witch or coven, how can he or she do so? What kind of altar should be set up, what basic tools would be required, and is there a nonsecret invocation that you could recommend?"

Part of their answer was: "Let's look at it this way: suppose a person in Lower Ipswich, Iowa, wanted to be a Catholic but could not attend a Catholic Church. Would she then have the right to conduct her own mass, baptize, hear confessions and so forth? I suppose she could do it and nobody would come to arrest her, but would such rituals have any validity in the eyes of the Church and would the self-proclaimed 'priest' have any status within the Church? Yes, I know that Jesus wasn't ordained, but he claimed a privilege which few others have claimed of late. It would be the same with someone who cannot contact a coven."

The Crowthers say: "Only a witch can make a witch,"

but do point out that one may practice paganism, since it is not as rigid as the craft. However, my question was not about Witches, valid or invalid, but about people who "want to worship the ancient deities." And it is irrelevant to ask if this would have validity in the eyes of the Church or other Witches. The question is: Is it relevant to our God and Goddess?

L.L.M.

7

Witchcraft Ceremonies

The first of these rites is for Halloween. It is based upon the ancient rite described in Chapter 5, and can be worked by one person on his own.

For this, a small caldron, or similar metal pot is required. The vessel is used to contain a fire which is to be lighted on the altar, so it is as well to place inside the container a coil of asbestos rope which is then saturated with methylated spirits.

The circle is set, as in the previous rites, and a bath taken. The circle is drawn, purified and scented, as before. The sacrifice is made, and the Goddess is invoked. Her stang is set up in the center of the circle. The reason for this ceremony is to bid farewell to the Goddess and welcome the God who is about to take over for the winter months.

First, the Goddess must be thanked for her help and the blessings received during the period over which she presides. "O Great Mother! Green Goddess of the forests and woods, the countryside and fields. I offer thee thanks for the fruits of trees and bushes, the grain from the fields and the fertility of cattle; for all things you have produced from your goodness so that we all may live and grow in strength. Also for the help you have given me in my magic work. Accept these goods which man has grown with your aid."

When this is said, a few different kinds of fruit and vegetables, along with a few ears of corn, are placed upon the altar. Afterward, these articles should be buried in the ground as a libation.

After a few minutes of meditation, the following "Farewell to the Goddess" should be recited.

> Farewell Great Mother, fair and dear;
> Return to us again next year,
> When you are rested by your sleep,
> Beneath the snow so white and deep.
> When shoots break through in April rain,
> Green Goddess please return again.
> Until the storms of Winter cease,
> Dear Lady sleep in perfect peace.

After bowing and raising your hand in the sign of Farewell, replace the stang of the Goddess with that of the God, and welcome him with the following verse:

> All hail! Old Hornie, bring thy wind,
> And in the wild chase hunt the hind.
> As, by the fire, we hear the blast,
> And shiver till the hunt has passed.

O ye, who seek the death of man,
Please spare as many as you can.
Be sparing with the wind that chills,
And brings with it so many ills.
Protect us from the snow and rain,
So we can till the land again,
And dig the earth and turn the sod.
Be kind to us O Dreaded God.

(We have mentioned that Europe has many legends of
the wild hunter who was the Horned God. Eric Maple
relates, in *The Realm of Ghosts,* how the peasants of
Brittany bolted their doors when the wild wind
howled, because this meant that the demon hunter was
abroad. Maple tells how one peasant was said to have
shouted: "Huntsman share your spoils," and half a
corpse fell down the chimney and landed in the hearth.

We have met many country people who still say
the "huntsman is abroad" when a howling wind blows.
We can easily imagine the shrieks of the wild hunter,
and similar noises, when the wind howls through the
trees and houses. The legend that he hunts human
beings comes from the fact that such treacherous
weather often causes the death of old people, coupled
with folk memory of the Horned God of Hunting and
Death.)

If you desire to try and contact friends who have
passed over, you must ask the God's help in this
matter:

O Horned One, Great Lord of Death,
I ask of you with bated breath,
To send me from your realm above,
A word from those we knew and love.

So once more let us all unite,
In conversation on this night,
And with each other laugh and smile,
For just a very little while.

By sitting in meditation one can often receive messages from people we once knew and were very close to. One can also use the Ouija Board, or any other method used by spiritualists. On such occasions, Patricia has had very good results with automatic writing. If nothing comes through, do not worry. In necromancy you cannot contact the dead every time you try, but departed spirits will always make contact if they have something important to say. Remember that they have the same difficulty in contacting us as we have in contacting them. As Halloween is the feast of the dead, one is more likely to get results then than at any other time. Even our folk memory makes everyone associate this night with witches and ghosts. This proves that the old people could contact the dead.

CANDLEMAS

The caldron, prepared as before, should stand in the center of the circle, and the altar should be decked with flowers. Wild ones are best; in fact, the dandelion, which is one of the first flowers to bloom in our countryside, was, in the Isle of Skye, Scotland, the sacred flower of the Goddess. There she was known by her Celtic name, Bridget.

In this rite, the candlesticks should be placed just inside the circle so that the circle is not broken when lighting them. One should use a taper so that they can all be lighted from the same flame. The circle must be cast and the primary rites carried out, as before.

Stand before the altar and say: "I give thanks to thee, O Dreaded One, for keeping me from harm during the dark days of your reign, and wish you well on your journey back to the underworld."

(The word *underworld* comes from the ancient days when people thought that the earth was flat, and that the underside was inhabited by the gods.)

Lift up the God stang, and hold it aloft, saying: "Depart now from this circle, and take with you the darkness and all sicknesses of winter."

Then hold the stang in both hands and cast it out of the circle: "Depart! Depart! Depart!"

Light the candle on the altar, saying:

> Vanish winter. Come in spring.
> Bring light and life to everything.
> Wake up from the wintery night!
> Revel in the springtime light.

At this moment, light the taper from the altar candle, and go around the circle lighting the four candles, saying: "Light! Light! Light! Light!"

Then go over to the caldron and plunge the taper into it. As it bursts into flames, call out: "Hail to the spring with its light and life."

Take up the Goddess stang and hold it aloft, saying: "Welcome to thee Green Goddess. Welcome to thee Great Mother. May thou soon become big with pregnancy and give birth to the fruits of the orchards, the corn of the fields, and the flowers of the countryside. May all the cattle follow your example and give birth to my young. Hail to thee Goddess of the land!

Hail to thee Goddess of the sea! Hail to thee queen of the time of flowers! May your light spread over the whole world and bring forth fine harvests."

The stang is then stood up, and after a short meditation, the following prayer is recited:

O Lovely Goddess, Queen of Spring,
Bring beauty forth in everything.
May plants and flowers develop soon,
From seeds we planted at full Moon.
O Goddess whom we all adore,
Protect and guide us evermore.
So mote it be.

As a symbol of the beginning of the season of sowing, some seeds should be planted in a pot of earth. This should be kept and used for other festivals. If the seeds grow well, it is looked upon as a good omen.

This is followed by the dance of fertility. A pole, or broom, is used as a hobbyhorse, and the witch prances around the circle and jumps in the air, shouting:

The higher we jump, the higher they grow.
Around, and around and around we go.

This is repeated over and over again, until one gets tired or giddy. This is sympathetic magic—the pole, or broom, is a phallic symbol, and the seeds will follow the actions of the dancer and grow high.

Another song for dancing is as follows:

Merrily around we go,
As we till, and as we sow.
Plant the new seeds in a row,

Up and down, and to and fro.
Scatter seeds about the field,
To ensure a bumper yield.
Dig and sow and plough and hoè,
As up and down the field we go.
Silver Moon shine up above,
Song birds sing your songs of love.
Everyone should dance and sing,
It is the merry time of spring.

This should be sung in a lighthearted and happy mood.
The circle is then closed in the usual manner.

LAMMAS

This is the time for giving thanks to the Great
Mother for causing the crops to grow. It is the time
when the harvesting begins, and the first sowings have
been gathered.

A tankard of cider should be placed upon the altar.
(We are suggesting cider because it is the old national
drink of our country folk, but ale or any other country
drink can be used.) Ears of corn, and wildflowers of the
season should be used as decorations. If one is lucky
enough to have a "corn dollie' (doll made of corn) this
should be placed in the center of the altar.

All preliminary rites are carried out as usual.

The stang of the Goddess is stood up. She is
invoked with the magic wand in the manner previously
described. The incense is held aloft between both
hands: "O Mighty Goddess, as the perfume from this
incense permeates this temple, so do the flowers that
thou hast caused to grow from the seeds we planted
scent the country air."

If the seed that was planted in the previous rite has grown, it should have been placed upon the altar; in which case, it should be held up and offered to the Goddess: "This seed, which I planted in your honor, has grown into this flower by the aid of the sun and moon and the gentle rain from the heavens which you have sent to enable our crops to grow. I place it on your altar in your honor. Blessed be."

This is followed by the song of the harvest. The tune is traditional *Harvest Song*

We've gathered the crops and we've har-
   vested the corn.
We've worked and we've toiled from the first
   light of morn.
The wheat's in the barn and the last root is up,
So now is the time to take cider and sup.

Our labor has ended, it's now time to rest.
The Goddess has given us all of the best.
I lift up the tankard and call for a toast,
To the Goddess of Summer, the one we love
   most.

She's given us fruit, and she's given us wheat.
She's given us all the good things we can eat.
The crops from the earth and the fish from
   the sea.
So drink up a toast to the Goddess with me.

Unless one wishes to work some magic, the circle should be closed in the usual manner.

BELTANE (MAY EVE)

Since this is the time when vegetation begins to grow, the altar should be decorated with May flowers and branches that are beginning to bud. The seed planted at Candlemas should be on the altar, also a small container of water. The caldron should be ready to light, at the edge of the circle.

This is a happy rite, and should be worked in a lighthearted manner. The pot of seeds is held up and the following song sung. It is sung to the tune of "Here We Come Gathering Nuts in May," which was a very ancient May festival song, and which has come down to us as a children's singing game.

> I planted this seed at Candlemas, at Candlemas,
>   at Candlemas.
> I planted this seed at Candlemas, so will you
>   fertilize them?
> O Gentle Goddess hear my plea, O hear my plea,
>   O hear my plea.
> And please do all you can for me, and help to
>   fertilize them.
> [Here you water the seed.]

Light a taper from the altar candle and thrust it into the caldron. (This action being symbolic of the sex act.) "I kindle this need fire in honor of the Queen of May, and add part of myself to the burning embers." (Cut some pubic hair, as previously done, and drop it into the burning caldron. The ancients always used body hair for sacrifices; not blood, as some think. This hair is part of the human being, and a growing thing. Blood can only be obtained by a certain amount of pain, and the loss of blood is part of killing, which does not go with a fertility cult. Any blood that was ever used had to be menstrual blood, called "Moon blood," which comes freely from the female body, and, in itself is part of fertility.)

Then dance around the circle, jumping over the caldron every time you pass it. This should be continued until the fire has died down.

May Song
Dance! Dance! And welcome in the May.
Dance! Dance! And let us all be gay.
Merrily we dance, and welcome to the Queen.
The Goddess of the country, the Goddess that is
    green.

Dance! Dance! And jump the Beltane fire.
Dance! Dance! Over the blazing pyre.
As high as we jump, the wheat must grow as tall.
Hail to the Goddess, Great Mother of us all.

Dance! Dance! And let us all be glad.
Dance! Dance! Maytime is never sad.
Colors from the rainbow that comes out with the
    showers,
Are taken by the sun and given to the flowers.

Dance! Dance! It is the start of May.
Dance! Dance! The time for us to play.
The Goddess of the country is the Goddess that is
    green.
So hail in the Maytime and welcome to its Queen.

Maytime prayer:

"O Green Goddess of the fields and woodlands, may the joy that we give out at this time stay with us throughout the whole year, and spread to all other creatures of this land. May the act of passing through the fire purify and enlighten me. And may it bring me luck in health wealth and happiness. So mote it be."

Unless one intends to work magic, close the circle in the usual manner.

8

Partial List of Principal Goddesses

Adamah	Semitic goddess later masculinized into "Adam"
Anaitis	Persian fertility goddess
Andred	Witch goddess, Forest of Weald, England
Aphrodite	Greek goddess of love
Aradia	Diana's daughter, founder; witch cult on earth
Artemus	Ancient Greek moon goddess
Arrianrhod	Welsh mother goddess
Asherali	Canaanite moon goddess of fertility
Ashtoreth	Phoenician moon goddess of fertility
Astarte	Fertility-moon goddess worshiped by Greeks, Romans
Beltis	Queen of the heavens
Bensozoa	Goddess name used in 12th-century France
Bona Dea	Goddess of homosexual women
Brigid	Celtic mother goddess of threefold muse; also Bride

Centeotle	Mexican goddess of Fertility
Ceres	Roman goddess of harvest, same as Greek Demeter
Ceridwen	Celtic fertility goddess
Chloris	Greek goddess of flowers
Cihuacohutl	Ancient Mexican fertility goddess
Cotyteo	Athenian goddess of Licentiousness
Cunti	Hindu goddess of Fecundity
Cybele	Moon goddess, great mother of ancients
Demeter	Mother of Persephone, Greek; same as Roman Ceres
Dew	Athenian goddess of fertility
Diana	Ancient Roman moon goddess
Duryu-Kali	Hindu phallic goddess, consort of Siva
Epona	Horse-faced goddess of Gaul
Flora	Roman goddess of flowers
Frea, Freya	Main Scandinavian earth goddess; also Frigga
Gaea	Ancient Greek earth mother goddess
Habondia	Goddess known as lady of love; also Lady Habonde
Hecate	Witch goddess of moon, called queen of night
Hera	Pagan goddess of marriage and pregnancy
Herodias	Roman goddess identified with Diana
Hertha	Ancient German mother-earth goddess
Io	Deified priestess of Hera; represents moon, female principle
Isa	Scandinavian goddess
Ishtar	Babylonia goddess of love, fertility
Isis	Ancient Egyptian moon goddess
Izanami	Japanese goddess of creativity
Jana	Roman moon goddess; Diana; Neapolitan witches are called Janara
Juno	Roman moon and earth goddess, queen of the heavens
Kivai-Yin	Japanese and Chinese queen of the heavens
Kivan-Non	Japanese version of Venus

Libera	Roman goddess of freedom
Lucina	Roman moon goddess, presided over pregnant women
Mani	Ancient Scandinavian moon goddess
Morrigan	Celtic goddess of death, similar to Hecate; also Morgan
Mut	Egyptian fertility goddess
Mylitta	Babylonian fertility goddess to whom women sacrificed virginity
Nut	Egyptian sky goddess
Ops	Roman fertility goddess; wife of Saturn
Pallas	Goddess of war and wisdom
Parvati	Hindu moon goddess
Persephone	Greek queen of underworld; Demeter's daughter; Roman Proserpina
Pertunda	Pagan goddess of sexual intercourse
Rhea	Ancient earth goddess
Rhiannon	Celtic-Welsh mother goddess
Sarasvati	Hindu goddess, wife of Brahma
Seb	Egyptian earth-mother goddess
Semele	Fertility goddess of the Semites
Shala	Consort of the sky-god Vul
Shing-Moo	Chinese goddess of the heavens
Siri	Hindu goddess, consort of Vishnu
Sita	Hindu equivalent of Persephone
Tlazolteotl	Mexican goddess of love
Um	Hindu goddess, wife of Siva; represents female principle
Venus	Roman goddess of love
Xochiqultzal	Mexican fertility goddess
Xochitecatl	Mexican goddess of generation

9

The Witches Tarot Cards

The following twenty-two major arcana cards were designed especially for use in the circle by Arnold Crowther, and are based upon witchcraft symbolism. Arnold originally made two packs which he painted by hand: one for the Sheffield coven, and the other for Doreen Valienti, the Witch of Brighton. This is the first time that these cards have been produced in any book on the craft. The meanings are also based on craft symbolism and have been proved most effective by those who have used them.

NOTE: Initiated Witches and students of witchcraft will immediately recognize much of craft symbolism in these cards. In most decks, card IX is depicted as The Hermit; here it is called The Elder, and is recognizably the late Gerald B.

Gardner. Card I in other decks is given as The Magician; here it is The Sorceress, as befitting those who worship the Mother Goddess and the female principal. Card III in other decks is The Empress; here it is the Shelah-Na-Gig, a grotesque fertility figure found engraved in many old Irish and English Christian churches, stemming from a time when the ancients celebrated sex and venerated reproduction. Card IV in other decks is The Emperor; here it is The Green Man. More precisely, this is a representation of the Cerne Giant, a male fertility figure associated with Helith, Helios or Hercules. In other decks card V is called The Hierophant, a fully dressed authoritarian figure vaguely resembling the Pope; here he is simply a naked high priest in keeping with the Gardnerian craft tradition. Card VI of The Lovers is frankly more intimate than other such depictions. Card VII, The Chariot, features a man at the helm in other decks; here it is a woman. Card XII is The Hanged Man in other decks; in the Witches' Tarot it is called Sacrifice, showing a male initiate being scourged by a high priestess.

Unlike other decks in which Death is usually depicted as a skeleton dressed as a knight—the grim reaper—here, in card XIII, it is shown as Cernunnos, the stag-antlered god of hunting, winter and the underworld. Card XVI, The Tower, depicts the powers of an old Witch, the hag or crone. True to craft tradition, card XVIII, The Moon, depicts the Goddess in her triple aspect—maiden, mother and crone—with three symbols showing the waxing, full and waning moon. One holds an athame, the other a scourge and the last a torch or candle. Card XIX, The Sun, features Stonehenge with the radiant sun in the background. Card XX, called The Judgment in other decks is named Rebirth in the Witches Tarot, in keeping with the Witch belief in reincarnation, showing a sky-clad young maiden resurrected in Summerland. In other decks, card XXI is called The World, but here it is given as The Green Goddess. We say Mother Earth, Mother Nature, Virgin Territory, Mother Church, and refer to various vehicles, such as ships, in the feminine gender. Card O, The Fool, usually shows a young man in other decks stepping dangerously close to a precipice. Here it depicts a Christian priest or minister with open Bible in his hands, ready to walk into oblivion!

If you wish to use this deck for divination, we suggest that you supplement it with a study of Dr. Martello's book *Understanding the Tarot*, in which the Arthur Edward Waite deck, designed by Pamela Colman Smith, is used. This will enable you to make comparisons of the two decks as well as helping you with more extensive and updated interpretations. Although not reproduced in this book, the Witches Tarot also has a Minor Arcana consisting of fifty-six cards, all designed with the same Witch symbolism and originality as the Major Arcana depicted here. The full deck will soon be available to the public.

L.L.M.

MEANINGS OF THE CARDS

I. THE SORCERESS

Awakening of one's true will. Realization of one's power that can be achieved by magic. You can achieve great things if you will continue to work at it, and put all your power and energy into it.

II. THE HIGH PRIESTESS

Something will be revealed to you. Secrets. Wisdom. A woman of authority can advise and help you.

III. SHELAH-NA-GIG

Fertility. Abundance. Growth. Fruitfulness. Action will achieve great results.

IV. THE GREEN MAN

Power. Authority. Will. Stability. A great person, or a person with authority.

V. THE HIGH PRIEST

Inspiration. The querist will meet a man who

can advise, and guide him, or her. A man with a certain amount of authority.

VI. THE LOVERS

Attraction. Love. Beauty. You will meet a faithful friend. It can predict a marriage, or the finding of a life-long friend or partner.

VII. THE CHARIOT

Triumph over enemies. Success in things attempted on your own.

VIII. JUSTICE

Triumph for the deserving person in a law case. If you are right you will succeed in the end, despite all opposition.

IX. THE ELDER

Proceed with caution. Seek advice from a sage. Do not spurn advice from older people. Seek knowledge from one who is an expert on the subject.

X. WHEEL OF FORTUNE

You may have your ups and downs, but success will finally come your way. Destiny. Luck and success.

XI. STRENGTH

Things can be altered to benefit you by your own power. One who may harm you can be prevented by gentleness and subtle means.

XII. SACRIFICE

You will have to submit willingly to some sort of sacrifice to gain what you require.

XIII. DEATH

A complete renewal or start of some project. Take special care of your health in bad weather. One can always avoid the hunter.

XIV. TEMPERANCE

Economy. Moderation in all things is necessary. Do not take on too many things at the same time or you may fall between two stools.

XV. THE DEVIL, or BAPHOMET

You must break away from being tied to your own failings or emotions, as they are not for the best. Magic and occult science. What is thought to be evil in the eyes of some people may be for the best. Something that is predestined but not necessarily evil. The animal instinct may come to the fore.

XVI. THE TOWER

Distress, adversity, or calamity. An accident may be caused by some other person.

XVII. THE PENTACLE

Hope and bright prospects. Spiritual uplift. Eternal youth and beauty.

XVIII. THE MOON

Occult forces which can work for or against you. Secret matters. Emotional upheavals. Fluctuation.

XIX. THE SUN

Material happiness. Contentment. Fortunate marriage. Successful sex life.

XX. REBIRTH

Complete change, usually for the better. One could have a new occupation or a new way of life. The past, with its worries and disappointments is now over. Things that have been dormant for some time will rise up again, and there will be good prospects for a successful finish.

XXI. THE GREEN GODDESS

Assured success in all things that are attempted. You may change your occupation or dwelling place for something far better. For those who till the land, a bumper harvest can be expected. Good results can be expected by making use of your own abilities.

O. THE FOOL

Folly. Pride comes before a fall. If you continue to act as though you are far superior to others you will have a setback and become a laughing stock in the eyes of other people. Keep your head out of the clouds and your feet firmly on the ground. Do not daydream.

USING THE CARDS

The full coven method. Shuffle the cards well and cut three times.

Deal out twelve cards in a circle, starting in the east. Reshuffle the remaining cards and pick out one. Place this in the center.

Turn the cards face up and begin reading from the first card dealt. The center card will give you the final result.

In this witches' pack there is no alternate meaning for reversed cards, as this is negative thinking, and there is no place for this in magick.

THE SORCERESS

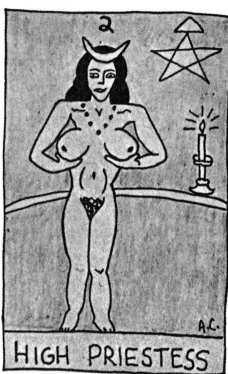

HIGH PRIESTESS

THE GREAT MOTHER

THE GREEN MAN

HIGH PRIEST

THE LOVERS

THE CHARIOT

JUSTICE

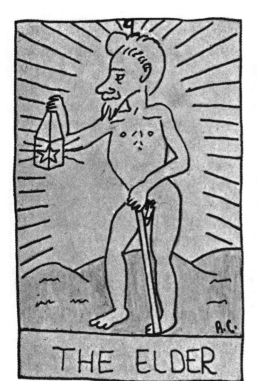

THE ELDER

THE WHEEL

STRENGTH

SACRIFICE

DEATH

TEMPERANCE

BAPHOMET

THE TOWER

THE STAR

THE MOON

THE SUN

REBIRTH

THE WORLD

THE FOOL

10

Psychometry—A
Power of the Witch

The old witch was often called the village wisewoman, and we know that the word *witch* came from the Anglo-Saxon word meaning wise. But how did these people gain their wisdom, especially when most of them were uneducated and could neither read nor write?

Let us take, for example, their knowledge of herbs. How was this knowledge obtained? How did they know which plant would cure what ailment? The idea of trial and error can be ruled out, as it is unlikely that the villagers would willingly act as guinea pigs and take a chance of losing their lives.

I believe that a great deal of the witches' knowledge came from their ability to use what is now called psychometry, which is being able to translate, by touch, the auras given off by all objects.

This theory came to me after I had seen a psycho-metrist "read" a bottle of pills. Although it was handed to him by a man, he was able to say that it really belonged to a woman, and gave a fairly good descrip-tion of her. He also described the chemists where it came from, but he was unable to say anything about the doctor who had prescribed them, as he said the medical man had never handled the bottle. By remov-ing the pills, he was able to say that the patient was taking them because she had high blood pressure. All the details were confirmed by the man who had presented the bottle.

After the demonstration, I asked the psychome-trist if I gave him some sprigs of herbs could he tell me what illnesses they would cure? He said he knew nothing about herbs or medicine, but that he would have a try. The following week, I brought him four cuttings of different herbs. I made a note of what he told me, and the following day, I checked it at the local library. In all four cases he was correct. Some of the herbs could be used for more than one illness, but I feel sure that the psychometrist would have discovered this if he could have spent more time on them.

When I told him of my theory about the old witches, he believed that I was on the right line, as he thought the art must have been practiced from very early times, and that being closer to nature than we are, the old people got better results, especially when touching natural things like herbs. In such cases, they would only be dealing with primary auras, whereas he had to deal with many extra auras which had been grafted onto the objects by various people who had worn or used them.

It is many years since I first saw a demonstration

of psychometry, but it still remains in my memory as if it was only yesterday.

It was at a dinner party that I was introduced to a middle-aged man by the name of Hemmingway. Hemmingway had a very likeable nature, was on the stout side, and wore a hearing-aid, though even with this device he had great difficulty in hearing. It turned out that he was an amateur psychometrist, so when the ladies went off together for a spell of women's talk, our host persuaded him to demonstrate his occult powers.

He asked for some article, and one of the guests handed him a pocket watch. After holding it in his hand for several minutes, Hemmingway informed the owner that the watch originally belonged to his grandfather, and then went on to describe the old gentleman. The owner of the watch admitted that he had described his relation perfectly.

As I have always been interested in conjuring, I thought there must be a trick in it somewhere. I suspected that Hemmingway had guessed from the type and age of the timepiece, that the man whose watch it was wasn't the first owner. I also believed that his description of the grandfather was guesswork, as men of that period were very much alike; many of them wore beards, and there wasn't a great difference in the way they dressed. I remembered how my own mother had an old photograph of her father and his four brothers; they all wore beards and frock coats, and it was all she could do to pick out her own father.

Next, Hemmingway took a ring from a friend of mine, and said it had been given to my friend by a relative. My friend admitted he had received it from an aunt. Hemmingway, still holding the ring, closed his eyes, and it was several minutes before he spoke again.

When he did, he described a cottage in the country which was next door to a farm. Then he said that he saw a donkey standing by the cottage door, and was certain that the animal had only one eye.

This naturally caused a laugh, and my friend said that although he could not say if the description of the cottage was right or wrong, he was certainly born in the country, and had lived there until he was five years old, when the family moved up to London. He certainly knew nothing about a one-eyed donkey.

Our host next offered a fountain pen which was a recent birthday present from his wife, Ann. This article seemed to give the psychometrist some difficulty, maybe because it was new. For a while, he could get nothing, then, all of a sudden, he said: "I can only get an impression of something green. Does it mean anything to you?" Our host smiled: "I was playing golf yesterday and got on the green in three strokes." "I don't think it has anything to do with that," laughed Hemmingway. "I think it's some sort of green material."

Just then, the door opened and the ladies returned. My friend's wife was holding a green evening dress over her arm: "Look what Ann has given me," she said to her husband. "It's too small for her and it fits me perfectly."

All the men's eyes turned to the dress and then to Hemmingway. Ann noticed our amazement and asked why we looked so surprised. I told the ladies about the experiments in psychometry, and they asked Hemmingway if he would try something for them. He asked if he could try his powers on the dress, and it was quickly handed to him. Within a few minutes he described the rest of the garments that had been hanging up in the wardrobe with it. We all went up into the bedroom to check his statements. Out of some dozen garments he was only wrong about two of them. This was not surprising, as, from a man's point of view, the unusual colors and styles were not all that easy to describe, even for us who were looking at them. Perhaps a female psychometrist might have done better.

A few days later, I met my friend in the street. "By the way," he said. "You remember that chap telling us about a one-eyed donkey?" "Yes," I replied. "Well, I asked my mother about it. She said: 'You can't possibly remember that. You were not three at the time.' Then she went on to explain that when we lived in that country cottage, a donkey used to come from the farm next door, and she used to feed it with pieces of bread and sugar. And the amazing thing is—the donkey only had one eye."

This absolutely proved to me that Hemmingway wasn't guessing, and that there was more in psychometry than I had imagined. I began to study it.

As psychometry is purely a matter of mind, there is nothing to stop anyone from doing it; after all, we are all born with a mind. The mind power of some may be greater than that of others, but it is possible to develop it if one only sets out to do it. Some people believe that psychometrists are born and not made, or think it is a supernatural gift; this is not the case at all, it is just a matter of practice and then more practice. Unlike card reading and other occult arts, there is no great strain on the memory, such as learning the meanings of the cards, their different combinations, and so on. There is also no outlay before one begins the study. One just has to hold some object and let the mind do the rest.

After a while, the student will begin to see visions, or pictures, in a kind of dream form, and since everyone has dreams, everyone should be able to see something in his mind's eye with a certain amount of concentration. I have heard psychometry described as "controlled daydreaming," and this is not a bad description of it because the visions seen by those who practice it are registered on the same cerebral center as that on which dreams are registered. Some occultists call this the "etheric eye," while others have referred to it as the "soul's eye." They identify it with the pineal gland, which they say is in the middle of the brain on the level with the base of the nose. This is believed to be the receiving center of all visual impressions received by the spirit body, and remains with the spirit after death when it separates from the physical body. Some medical doctors think that the pineal gland may be the relic of a third eye which man had in the early stages of evolution. There are also stories of Tibetan lamas being able to develop this eye by an operation that pierces the skull at the top of the nose, but this sounds more like fiction than fact.

None of the above theories can be proved one way or the other, but we definitely know that psychometrists are able to see visions by one means or another. These visions are usually distinct, but they last no more than a few seconds, so the psychometrist must be quick in describing what he sees. If he delays too long, the picture will go before he can say much about it, and another one will have taken its place.

The size and nearness of the picture seems to vary with different people, and according to my investigations, some see them almost life-size, while others have told me that it is like looking through the wrong end of a telescope. Some say the visions they see are rather blurred, but this may be due to want of practice, or because they have not done it for some period and have lost a certain amount of power.

Whether psychometrists hear things or not is difficult to say. Personally, I never hear anything, but I have known those who do receive some sensation of sound and have described bands playing, birds singing, and even the sound of running water, thunder and explosions. Whether these people simply imagine the sounds from the pictures they see, I cannot say, but I have been told that some people have the same sensation of sound when dreaming. I have never had this experience, so I cannot describe what these people actually hear. They certainly do not receive sounds through their physical ears; Hemmingway, whom I have mentioned previously, said he often got sounds when holding different objects, and he was almost stone deaf.

Other people have told me that they get impressions of sounds but are not always able to say what makes them. This is not surprising, as we all have that difficulty in everyday hearing. If we are not familiar with what makes a certain sound, we can only guess at it, and may really be far off the mark. Few people, except musicians, could pick out more than a few instruments in an orchestra, and only experts can say what type of aircraft makes a particular sound. The ordinary person has a very limited knowledge of sounds, so one cannot expect a psychometrist to explain accurately every impression of sound he receives.

Some early writers on the subject have listed the requirements necessary for a would-be psychometrist; such as extreme sensitivity, a good education, a delicate regard for the feelings of others, a knowledge of geography, history, color, physiology, physiognomy, zoology and spirituality and a high moral personal standard.

This kind of list is enough to turn anyone away from attempting the art, though I am certain that the majority of psychometrists I have come across met very few of these requirements. In fact, one woman I met, who was very expert at it, could neither read nor write, had a tongue like a Billingsgate fish porter, and was always at loggerheads with her neighbors. I wouldn't say that the above requirements could not be helpful, but I wouldn't say they were really essential. I believe that excess smoking and drinking are bad for all occult working because they dull the senses, which should be very active when psychometrizing various articles. It is also advisable not to attempt psychometry soon after a heavy meal.

Dr. J. R. Buchanan, author of *A Manual of Psychometry*, who studied the subject for more than thirty years, believed that women made better psychometrists than did men. He said: "The superior delicacy of the female constitution renders the psychometrical faculty a much more common endowment of females than of males. A large proportion of females between the ages of sixteen and twenty evince psychometrical faculties."

This may be true, but I can only speak as I find,

and the majority of psychometrists I have met have been males. Perhaps this is because more men study the subject these days than they did when Dr. Buchanan was alive. I do not believe that sex has anything to do with it. I have met both men and women who have been in old houses and claimed they have sensed a strange atmosphere, either good or bad. This shows that both sexes have the nucleus for psychometry.

The theory of psychometry is that the human mental aura radiates in every direction, even outside the body, and impresses everything within its immediate orbit. All articles, no matter how solid they may appear to be, have minute holes in the surface, and these collect the minute particles of the mental aura of the people who have worn or used them.

If one psychometrizes a human being, one is nearer to the brain, or source of radiation, and should be able to obtain much better results than when one is holding something that has been used by that person, as only a very small portion of the the total vibrations are concealed in the article.

In some cases where experiments are being carried on in the presence of several "sitters," the vibrations given off by one of the people present may be stronger than those given off by the article. This can easily put the psychometrist off and lead him up the wrong path. The reading he gives may have nothing to do with the article, as he is really reading the aura of the person sitting near him. An experienced psychometrist may realize this, and would ask that person to sit further away or leave the room.

This happened once when I attended a demonstration where there was a minister present. The psychometrist just could not get anything right. He presumed that one of the sitters had a very strong aura and was working against him. He finally gave up altogether. After the fiasco, he mentioned his theory to the minister: "You are quite right," said the cleric. "I was doing it."

"Whatever for?" asked the psychometrist.

The minister spoke in a very serious manner: "Because I'm against all this witchcraft stuff. It's nothing but the work of Satan."

If an article has been left in a drawer for a long period, it is likely to pick up some of the auras of the other things that have been lying in the drawer with it. An example of this has already been described in the experiment of Hemmingway and the green dress.

Many people believe that the art of psychometry is a special gift; either magical or supernatural. This is a fallacy and is the reason why more people do not attempt it. This false image has been created by spiritualistic mediums who give the impression that their psychometry is caused by the aid of some spirit guide or other person who has passed over. There is nothing at all supernatural in the act; one might call it supernormal because it is in the makeup of everyone, but it has to be developed. Anyone with a normal mind can achieve it, providing one is in good health, not too young, and willing to practice. It is purely a matter of sensitivity, training and development.

Although many people may not agree with me, I believe that psychometry is the basis of nearly every occult practice, like fortune-telling, mindreading, mediumship and so forth.

In card reading, the consulter is always asked to shuffle the deck, and in doing so is certain to leave some of his aura on the cards. This is picked up by the cartomancer, and the information thus gained, combined with the meaning of the selected cards, will give a much more personal reading. I have gained this theory from personal experience. I have noted, when having the cards read by a professional reader, that the meaning of the cards had very little bearing upon myself, but the reader gave me information that could apply to no one else. It was obvious that she was taking no notice of the cards, and was obtaining her knowledge some other way—psychometrically.

People who consult mediums must be impregnated with a certain amount of the aura of their loved ones who have passed over; this is really what the medium is reading. Even palmists must receive vibrations from the hands they hold and this, combined with their knowledge of the lines, gives a more correct reading. I am sure that gypsy palmists depend upon psychometry when they are "reading" hands, as many that I have questioned know nothing or very little about the lines themselves, yet many of their readings are very true.

It has been said that all inanimate objects have a life and memory of their own. This applies especially to stones, which were once held to be sacred and to contain special spirits. Stones were always associated with religion and the old deities, and we still have many standing stones and stone circles all over the British Isles.

A psychometrist friend of mine spent several months psychometrizing the stones of the famous circle called the Rollright Stones, in Oxfordshire, and gained a great deal of information. He obtained considerable knowledge about the ancient religious and magical rites performed at such places; some of the information that I have given in the first part of this book was obtained through him.

It all goes to prove that psychometry has no bounds as far as time is concerned, and that through it we may gain information about things that happened many centuries ago. If more archaeologists studied the subject, we would no doubt be able to know much more about prehistoric man than we do at present.

Psychometry could also be used in crime detection. Imagine what could be learned from a murder weapon or other articles which are referred to in criminal courts as exhibits. Unfortunately, as the law stands, it is doubtful whether the evidence of a psychometrist would ever be accepted in court, and I don't think any police would act upon it either.

Bland mentions how a French doctor who was connected with a prison tried out a female psychometrist by letting her read some forty neckties taken from male prisoners. The. woman correctly described the appearance of each criminal, the crime he had committed and the sentence he received.

Although the Witchcraft Act of 1735 has been repealed, many people still think that those who have anything to do with the occult are rogues and vagabonds or, at least, extremely eccentric. I admit that anything savoring of the occult attracts many of the lunatic fringe, but often practitioners themselves help to add to the low rating of the art. They are not satisfied to present psychometry as a natural science, but insist they have some magical power, or achieve their results through spirits. Such people are either conscious or unconscious fakes, and can only harm genuine psychometrists.

Throughout the years that I have attended meetings of psychical research societies and spiritualists, I have seen many psychometrists. Some have been genuine, others seemed to know very little about the subject, while a few were complete frauds.

Let me give an example of how one such person worked. She was a middle-aged woman. She spoke in a very affected manner, but her frequent dropping of *h*'s showed it was a put on. She was a good showman, but her knowledge of psychometry was almost nil.

She first collected a large number of different objects, on a tray, from the audience. Then she mounted the platform and sat at a table with the tray in front of her. She closed her eyes and remained silent for a while. Then she asked for the lights to be lowered. After more concentrating, she spoke: "My spirit friends tell me that a John is trying to contact someone. Does anyone recall a person by that name who has passed over?"

Two people accepted the name. She asked if she had an article belonging to either of them. An elderly lady admitted she had: "Then it must be for you. What did you give me?" The woman told her, and she picked up a brooch: "I thought this was yours, I can feel your vibrations, I just wanted to make quite certain."

She held the brooch to her forehead and continued: "Was John a relation?"

"He was my husband," replied the woman.

"Yes. He is telling me that now. He gave it to you as a present."

"That is correct."

"My spirit guides tell me that you and your husband were very close."

"You are quite right. We loved each other very much."

The medium continued to fish around, giving information that could apply to anyone. Sometimes she gave advice: "My spirit friends say there is no need to worry," or, "My guide advises you to take things easy and rest."

The dear old ladies who sat in the dimly-lighted hall were fully convinced that they were in touch with the dead, and seemed to think that the fee they paid the medium was money well spent, but it was certainly not psychometry. I have seen more convincing demonstrations given by music hall mind readers, and they never professed to be anything but conjurers.

One of the simplest methods for starting the study of psychometry is to try it out on the letters you receive by mail. Without looking at the writing, hold the letter in your hand and make a note of whatever comes into your mind. At the beginning you may find that you get very little, but with continual practice you will find that you are able to tell the sex of the writer, and often what it is about. As letters pass through many hands before you receive them, it is perhaps better to open the envelope and try holding the letter without unfolding it. Sometimes the postman, or the sorter, has a stronger mental aura than the writer, and you may get the impression from the envelope that the writer is a male, when it is really a female.

It is no good making feeble attempts and then giving up. There is no such thing as instant psychometry; it is like becoming a musician or a juggler, you must go all out to do it and keep on practicing. If you are not willing to do that, it is best to forget about it altogether.

After you have experimented with letters, you should get a sympathetic friend to help you. Let him, or her, bring articles of which he knows the history. Sit comfortably in a chair, with your friend some distance away. Make sure that both your hands and the article are warm, and then gently rub the object with your fingers. Closing the eyes often helps beginners. Don't be self-conscious or nervous, and describe, as clearly as you can, all the impressions that you get. Do not carry on for more than half an hour without a break. Longer periods only cause fatigue, and the visions will get blurred and may not even refer to the object being psychometrized.

It is advisable, when starting, to use "one vibration" objects only; that is, articles that have had only one owner. These will be easier for the student, because he will not get confused by vibrations from a number of owners.

It has been said that the psychometrist, while handling an article belonging to a sitter, is temporarily living a part of the physical, emotional, mental and spiritual life of the owner of that article, as some of his mental aura has been absorbed by the article, giving the article an aura of its own. I have actually seen tears come into the eyes of a psychometrist, who was extremely sensitive, when she described a sad period in the life of the owner.

No good work can be done in a hurry. Rapid revelations may impress the audience, but this is not true psychometry. It takes time and patience to correctly describe the various pictures, or impressions, one receives, and undue haste often results in failure. Professionals are often expected to work under pres sure, so many of them often have to depend upon imagination and fiction.

After the student has finished with one article, he should rub his hands together, or wipe them with a handkerchief, before starting with the next one. This will remove any of the mental aura left on his hands by the previous object. Unless this is done, wrong statements may be made.

Gems, such as diamonds, are difficult to psychometrize, because they have passed through many different hands before finally being made, for example, into a ring. It has memories of the geological process which turned it into a diamond; of the workmen who took it from the earth; of the cutter, polisher, and the man who set it in the ring. Added to this are the diamond buyers, jewellers' assistants, and would-be customers who have handled it. It takes a very experienced psychometrist to sort all this out.

Articles that are worn next to the skin, like necklaces, bangles, and medallions, are by far the easiest things to psychometrize. Also, large beads and other things that have big surfaces. Finger rings and other small articles take a much longer time. Whether the article is made of a soft or hard material does not seem to matter. Handbags are very complicated, as they usually contain an array of articles and are constantly being put down on various surfaces—counters, tables, beds and so on. Coins pass through so many hands that they are almost useless for obtaining good results; one should refrain from accepting handkerchiefs and other articles that are frequently being washed.

Sometimes the student may think that his statements are not correct because the sitter refuses to accept them. One should not worry about this, as often the sitter will not acknowledge a statement simply because of his lack of knowledge of the history of the article, or because the event happened before the object come into his possession. No one can be expected to remember every event in his life, so correct, or incorrect, all impressions should be noted and confirmed or rejected.

Very soon, the beginner will find how much truth he can read from various articles, and this will encourage him to press on with his studies. As he finds himself improving, and getting better results, he may find a slight tendency to exaggerate when describing his visions. This should be guarded against.

The following example shows how easily an object with various mental auras attached to it may give off a reading that will be translated in different ways by different people, though both are right.

The psychometrist was given a statuette made of bronze. It represented a seated woman suckling a young child. The woman bore a disk headdress encircled by horns.

The reader described a sandy place with large palacelike buildings. It appeared to be a very sunny day, and he could see a river with boats on it. The people in the vision appeared to be wearing robes, and he received the name Isis.

The sitter knew nothing about the figure, except that he bought it in an antiques shop in the Lanes, Brighton, some years before. He accepted all the statements, and explained that the psychometrist must have been describing Brighton, but must have mistaken the sea for a river. The sand would have been the beach. He admitted that he had bought the statue during his summer holiday, and it was certainly very hot weather. The palacelike buildings would certainly be the Royal Pavilion, built by George IV. It all seemed to fit, yet one of those present threw a wrench in the works. He knew Brighton well. It had a very stony beach and not sand, and what did the name Isis mean?

The owner of the figure quickly changed his story. He knew what it all meant now. He had lived for some years at Oxford, and had often gone boating on the river Isis. What appeared to be palaces were really the university buildings, and the robed figures were the dons.

This all seemed to fit, but the true explanation went much further back than that. This was discovered when the owner took his relique to the British Museum to find out what it really was. It turned out to be of ancient Egyptian origin, and some 3000 years old. It was a figure of the Goddess Isis with the child Horus. The sun and sand which the psychometrist saw obviously represented the desert country of Egypt; the buildings were the ancient temples; the river was the Nile; and the robed people were the Egyptians themselves.

If either the psychometrist or the sitter had known anything about Egyptology, he would have been able to interpret the vision; but, on the other hand, the reader would have recognized what the figure represented and we might not have got such a good example of psychometry.

If only people would accept psychometry as a serious science, and more modern witches would study it, there is no doubt we would be able to learn a lot more about the ancient rites of witchcraft and magic.

11

Who Was Saint George?

Saint George was one of
the Heavenly Twins, or
Sons of Thunder, whose
cult at one time was distributed over the whole world.
These naked horsemen date back to many thousands
of years before Christ.

Legend tells us that they were river gods who went
to sea. They first taught men to build ships, hollowed
out of the sacred oak. They protected sailors from
danger and founded the first cities; invented the ox-
drawn plough of stone and wood; were dieties of
rejuvenation and promoted fertility in nature and man;
healed the sick, especially the blind; and appeared
upon battle fields as the harbingers of victory.

There were other such twins throughout the
world, and according to legend, the elder twin is

always divine and the younger one human, but the human twin always supplants the divine one.

Michael was the divine one, the heavenly messenger, and became patron of sacred mounts and midsummer and harvest festivals. George was the human twin, who played the humble role of representative of the agricultural workers, and possibly that of jester. The nature of the part he played in festival mimes survived in medieval Greece, and he was given the title The Drunkard; in Crete he became known as Mad Saint George on account of the license of his festival.

That there should be shrines to the Heavenly Twins both on the Bosphorus and the English channel at Troy and at London; that the name Michael was first found in Asia Minor, and that Saint George of England is George of Cappadocia, are all indications of a very strong link between Troy and Britain.

The Cross of Saint George can also be traced back to Asia Minor. The red cross of the Twins is one of the earliest religious symbols known to man. Nothing is more astonishing than that the Cross should come to be regarded as preeminently a Christian symbol. Bushmen and many Red Indian tribes make the sign of the cross to ward off evil spirits.

The red cross of the twins was always found on a white background, red and white being the color of the Twins.

London is essentially a city of the Twins. They will be found carved on the west pediment of Saint Paul's Cathedral, which is a shrine of the Order of Saint Michael and Saint George.

Many of their ancient attributes are very characteristic of Britain. They go to sea. They build ships. They heal the sick. Their red cross, incorporated in the

Union Jack, goes to war on land and sea, and the red cross flies over hospitals.

In Britain, the Heavenly Twins always appear in their ancient role as naked horsemen. On the medals of 1914–18, and on the now vanished gold sovereigns, it was Saint George who rode naked to fight the dragon. But until the Middle Ages it was not Saint George but Saint Michael who appeared as the naked horseman on English coins. The Michael mintage of Edward IV was also connected with some of the old attributes of the god Michael, for they were in great demand for touching in the miraculous cure of the King's Evil.

The change from the Michael mintage of the fourteenth century to the George mintage of the nineteenth reflects a change in Britain's patron saint, which is not generally realized. As material wealth in Britain began to increase and the country to become more and more a plutocracy, George, the human twin who inherited the material wealth, began to rise in importance. Finally, like Jacob, George usurped both birthright and the blessings from his divine brother.

Thus, today we have a somewhat absurd evolution wherein the jester and infamous Saint George has become transformed into the renowned Saint George of England.

Saint George's Day is a day of fertility rites.

Among the Slaves, a barren woman who desires to have a child places a new chemise upon a fruitful tree on the eve of Saint George's Day. The next morning before sunrise she examines the garment, and if she finds that some living creature has crept on it, she hopes that her wish will be fulfilled within the year. Then she puts on the garment confident that she will be as fruitful as the tree on which it spent the night.

Among the Slavs of Carinthia, on Saint George's Day, the young people deck with flowers and garlands a tree which has been felled on the eve of the festival. The tree is then carried in procession with music and laughter, the chief figure in the procession being Green George, a young fellow clad from head to foot in green birch branches. At the close of the ceremony, the Green George, that is an effigy of him, is thrown into the water. In many places, the lad himself is ducked in the river or pond, with the express intention of ensuring rain to make the fields and meadows green in summer. In some places, the cattle are crowned and driven from their stalls with the accompaniment of a song:

> Green George we bring.
> Green George we accompany.
> May he feed our herd well,
> If not, to the water with him.

A similiar ceremony took place among the gypsies of Transylvania. On the eve of Saint George's Day, a young willowtree was cut down, garlanded and set up in the ground. Women "with child" placed one of their garments under the tree and left it there overnight; if the next morning they found a leaf of the tree lying on the garment, they knew their delivery would be easy.

Sick and old people went to the tree in the evening, spat on it three times, and said, "You will soon die, but let us live." The next morning the Gypsies gathered around the willow tree. As in the previous ceremony, Green George appeared. He threw a few handfuls of grass to the cattle in order that they might not lack fodder throughout the year. Then he took three iron nails, which had lain three days and nights in water, and knocked them into the willowtree; after which he pulled them out and threw them into a running stream to propitiate the water spirit. The ceremony finished as before with Green George being thrown into the river.

In various parts of Europe customs have prevailed, both at spring and harvest, which are based on the notion that the sexual relation between man and woman can be used to quicken the growth of plants.

In the Ukraine, on Saint George's Day, the priest, in his robes and attended by his acolytes, goes to the fields of the village, where the crops are beginning to show green, and blesses them. After that, the young married people lie down in couples and roll several times over on them, with the belief that this will promote the growth of the crops.

In parts of Russia, the priest himself was rolled by women over the sprouting crop, without regard to the mud and holes which he might encounter on his beneficent progress. If he resisted or remonstrated, his flock cried out, "little Father, you do not really wish us well, you do not wish us to have corn, although you wish to live on corn."

PART II

A Witch Under Fire

Questions and Answers About all Phases of Witchcraft

A Witch Under Fire

Answers to questions that people ask about Witch-craft.

What does the word 'witchcraft' really mean?

Witchcraft is one of the most misused words in the English language, and has been wrongly used by authors and journalists to describe anything they are unable to explain—from ritual magic to vandalism in churchyards. If something is weird and inexplicable, then it must be witchcraft.

The real explanation is The Craft of the Witches, whose original title was The Wicca, from Anglo-Saxon, meaning "wise ones." So the true meaning is "the craft of the wise people." There is nothing evil or sinister about that.

Is Witchcraft a religion?

Yes. It is the original prehistoric religion of Western Europe. Its followers worshiped a horned god of hunting and death, and a mother goddess of fertility and rebirth. The Great Mother has been worshiped in every country from time immemorial, under different names, and even today, we speak about her as Mother Nature.

Witches believe in reincarnation, and hope they will be born again among their own people. When they die, they believe that they go to the "summerlands of the gods," where they are rested and purified before being reborn on this earth.

Is it true that reincarnation was once taught by Christians?

Yes. The early Christians taught it, and this can be proved by the words of Saint Gregory, Bishop of Nyssa: "It is absolutely necessary that the soul shall be healed and purified, and if it doesn't take place in one life on earth, it must be accomplished in future earthly lives."

Later, in A.D. 533, reincarnation was declared a heresy by the Council of Constantinople.

Why does the god of the Witches wear horns?

The most popular theory goes back to prehistoric times, when man had to hunt to live. As the bow and arrow had not been invented, beasts were killed by inciting them to stampede over precipices. To do this, a man would run among them, screaming and shouting. He was dressed in animal skins and wore a pair of horns on his head; this disguise enabled him to get nearer to the cattle, as the smell of the skin would hide the smell of a human being. This method of hunting is still used by some tribes to this day.

The man who acted as the decoy had to be very brave and would have been admired by the rest of the tribe; no doubt, he became the leader and took a chief part in the tribe's magic rites.

When prehistoric man conceived the idea of a god, he would obviously depict him as his ideal man; the ancient cave paintings show the god wearing skins and horns, like the brave hunter who enabled man to get food to live.

In the same way, Christian artists, throughout the ages, have painted pictures of Jesus as their ideal man. That is why pictures of him differ so much. Some have even given him blue eyes and fair hair and neglected the characteristics of the Eastern race. That was one reason why the statue of Christ by Jacob Epstein, exhibited first in 1920, caused so much controversy. Prehistoric man wasn't concerned about the features of his god as long as he had horns.

Later, horns became a symbol of power and were adopted by Romans, Danes and others to denote military rank. Even Michaelangelo put horns on his statue of Moses. Some say he did this because he confused the word for *horns* with that for *halo*. Others believe that Michaelangelo secretly belonged to the old religion and that his Moses is really a representation of the ancient god.

Horns are also a symbol of the crescent moon, and as witchcraft is a moon cult, they represented the Moon Goddess. The horned man could be a symbolic combination of the God and Goddess. This could be true, as many of the ancient gods were bisexual.

Why do Witches keep the names of their deities secret?

Witches never mention the names of their gods because they work magic in their names, and if outsiders got to know the names it would weaken the witches' power. It is the same as the modern superstition that if you tell someone your wish it will never come true. People who carry lucky charms and talismans will never show them to others or, if they do, they will lose their power.

This fact, I have discovered so often myself. Many times I have decided to do something or go somewhere, and when I have told others of my intentions, something has always happened to prevent my doing it. It has happened too many times to be just coincidence. Many of you must have experienced the same thing, and the old adage, "Never count your chickens before they are hatched," show it must be a pretty general thing.

In a more material sense, the society of conjurers called the "Magic Circle" insists that their members should not disclose the secrets of their tricks to the general public. They know that once the secret is known, the audience loses all interest and that they, themselves, will lose their power to mystify people.

Some of the ancients believed that if outsiders knew the names of the gods they would lure them away for themselves. Another reasonable explanation is that early witches used the gods' names to prove their membership of the cult; they were the passwords into the circle.

Why did Witches wear tall pointed hats?

As far as I know, there is no evidence they ever did. Perhaps it was an exaggeration of the hats worn by the Puritans, which was not unlike the Welsh national ladies' hat.

Early pictures of witches never show tall pointed hats. They just depict the witches wearing the regular costume of the period. The women are either hatless or they wear a cloth over their heads as modern women wear a scarf.

It is hard to discover when pointed hats first appeared in pictures of witches, but I should imagine it's fairly modern; perhaps around the Victorian era. Who invented them, or how they came to be invented, is just a matter of guessing.

A tall conical hat has always been associated with wizards, so perhaps some artist added a brim to turn it into women's attire, as a witch would be looked upon as a female wizard.

It was obviously started by some illustrator of fairy stories. Since the fairytale witch is always the wicked character, perhaps the woman in the tall black hat and a cloak was the female counterpart of "Sir Jasper" or some other villain of melodrama, who always wore a tall silk hat and a cloak. Perhaps the witches' big hooked nose corresponded to Sir Jasper's big black moustache.

It could be that the hooked nose was a phallic symbol, as the witch belonged to a fertility cult. This suggestion has also been put forward to account for Punch's similar nose, but I doubt if artists of childrens' books would go so deeply into the matter. I think it was just someone's idea to depict an evil woman and it caught on. Hence, the image of the witch was born. Elizabethan woodcuts never showed a witch as uglier than an ordinary woman, but unpleasant looking women would be disliked by children.

I was once told by a Punch and Judy man that he made a pretty Judy but the children objected to Punch knocking her about, so he had to go back to the ugly character. It is strange how people associate ugliness with evil. Perhaps that is why newspapers always print the worst pictures they can find of criminals. No one likes to convict a pretty or handsome person.

Another suggestion for the crooked nose was anti-Semetic, because often-persecuted Jews left the towns and went to live with the witches, who helped them with their ritual magic.

I have had two other suggestions given to me as an explanation of the tall pointed hat. One person suggested it was a fertility symbol; depicting the male and female principals. The circular brim represented the yoni and the tall conical crown the lingam symbol.

The second idea was that the brim represented the circle in which the magic rites took place, and the crown portrayed the "cone of power" that the witches raised by dancing in the circle. Both ideas are ingenious, but there is no proof that either is the correct answer.

Did Witches fly on broomsticks?

Anyone with a scientific mind will know this is impossible, but there is no smoke without fire, so there must have been something that gave rise to this superstition.

Witches practiced an old fertility rite to make the crops grow, which necessitated the use of a pole as a hobbyhorse and dancing around the field as they sung the following jingle:

The higher we jump, the higher they grow.
Around and around and around we go.

This was repeated over and over again, and the crops were supposed to follow suit and grow high. This is an example of sympathic magic. A simple jingle was used so that the witches didn't have to think about what they were saying, and it registered on their subconscious minds.

Television advertisers use jingles in the same way, so that with constant repetition, the names of their wares become implanted in the minds of their would-be customers, and so that when consumers want something in this line, they automatically ask for that make. The idea of putting new words to well-known songs helps a lot, as the tune is already in the subconscious mind. Very few people know the tune of "Scotland the Brave," but they will hum it to you if you call it "Scots' Porridge Oats." In the olden days this would have been looked upon as magic.

The dancing pole was a phallic symbol, and a witch on a pole represented the male and female principals. It may have been a forerunner of the Maypole, which is also a phallic emblem—the pole being male, and the circle of dancers female. Even today, the Maypole dancers are always girls. Neither the Maypole dance nor the hobbyhorse pole dance should be performed by males, or the symbolism is completely lost. During the days of the witch-hunts, it would be dangerous to have a dancing pole in the house, as it might lead to conviction, so the witches took to using broomsticks. This would pass unnoticed, or if it was discovered, no witch-finder could convict a woman for having a necessary domestic article.

The word *flying* is often used very loosely, when *running* or *going very fast* would fit the situation better. You often hear people say, "He was flying down the road," or, "I must fly now." You don't expect these people to take off into the air, so it is reasonable to suppose that people who saw the pole or broomstick dance, also said, "I saw the witches flying along on their broomsticks," instead of saying, "I saw them galloping along with a broomstick between their legs."

Some people have put forward a suggestion that the witches hypnotized people to "see" them flying through the air, in the same way that others have tried to explain the Indian Rope Trick by mass hypnotism. This has been proved untrue as far as the rope trick is concerned, so it is, most probably, untrue about the witches.

Once an artist had drawn a picture of a woman flying on a broomstick, many people would believe it was true. In one of my television interviews, the producer made me disappear, by clever camera work, and I had many letters from people offering to buy *my* secret of dematerialization; and we are living in the age of science!

Do Witches believe in black magic?

Magic is neutral; it can be used for good or evil, but no respectable witch would use it for evil. Witches believe in a kind of Karma, that evil returns on the evil-doer, and wouldn't take these chances.

Do you think that sticking pins in a wax figure would hurt anyone?

I doubt it. It certainly wouldn't work if the person who was being hexed didn't know about it. If he did, it might have some effect on him; in which case, he should blame himself as much as the person who was doing it for believing such nonsense.

I believe that people of the olden days were hoaxed by the idea of black magic. Nobody likes to be a failure or is willing to take the blame for everything. Black magic became a scapegoat for their failings. It was easier to say, "My crops have been bewitched," than to admit the crops had failed by neglect and laziness.

Doctors were not so skilled in those days, so they could blame black magic for their own ignorance! Death was always thought to be the result of witch-craft, so if the patient died, the people would imagine that the witch had greater powers than the doctor. If the doctor cured the patient, he could say his medical skill beat the magic of the witch. Whatever happened, he was always in the right, and even the bereaved relatives would believe that no human could work against the Devil. They could always put their hands on someone they believed would work black magic against the dead man, for there is no one born who hasn't an enemy somewhere; especially the rich and those who achieve fame.

If the pin-sticking operation really worked, people

would be dropping dead all over the place, and everyone would be scared of their neighbors and relations. Wars wouldn't be necessary, and the nation that had the most wax and pins would win every time.

When the belief in black magic was widened, people with guilty consciences began to have qualms as soon as anything went wrong or they became ill. They thought at once that someone was working against them. It was only those who had done evil to others who believed that *others* were trying to destroy *them*. These, like James I, helped to spread the rumors of black magic.

It soon became a state of mind. It had come to stay. Commercially minded people saw there was money to be made in this new "gimmick," so they peddled antiwitchcraft charms and potions; became witch-doctors and witch-finders. In England, people like Mathew Hopkins, the self-styled witch-finder general, was paid twenty shillings for every woman convicted of practicing witchcraft; and in those days, a pound was really worth having. He also sold witchcraft antidotes, and if people wouldn't buy them, he knew they were on the side of the witches, and convicted them. He received money both ways.

People in those days must have been well brainwashed to make laws about something that only existed in the minds of the gullible peasant folk; but there was money in it and witch-finding became "big business." If this hadn't been the case, the whole thing would have been a nine-day wonder; but witches meant money, so they had to be found and destroyed. The general public flocked to these hangings and burnings as they do to football matches today. Witch-hunting swept the country as "Bingo" has in this modern age.

Did the people who worked black magic believe in it themselves?

This I cannot say. It certainly gave them power in the eyes of the villagers. Many a poor old woman was executed just because she lived alone, kept a cat and was disliked by her neighbors. The only power she really had was that bestowed upon her by the villagers.

From an obscure person she was raised to fame and her supposed magic powers were feared by all the inhabitants. There is no doubt that many old crones, having tasted for the first time in their lives, power and fame, confessed to dealings with the Devil and other ridiculous things that were put into their mouths by the inquisitors. As many of them were almost at the end of their lives, they might have thought it was far better to finish it in the limelight of notoriety than to die the lonely death of an unwanted person.

So many people love to have power over others, and the belief in black magic gave them that power. The African witch-doctor may not believe it himself, but as long as the rest of the tribe believe it, he will remain all-powerful.

Have you ever met a black magician?

Yes; or at least people who *claim* they are black magicians. They are usually insignificant people who want publicity in the press or on television. They are usually expert liars, gather round them a few of the lunatic fringe and have no power at all. If you ask them to demonstrate their powers, you will find it is always the wrong time or the planets are in the wrong position. They always have a good excuse for not doing anything, but they won't admit their magic doesn't work. If you ask them to make a wax figure of you and stick pins into it, it calls their bluff. These people are either kidding you or themselves, or are completely phony.

What about Gypsy curses?

The old saying, "Sticks and stones will break my bones but words won't ever hurt me," is very true. Gypsy curses and evil spells have never hurt anyone and never will. If they harm you, blame yourself and not the Gypsy. The only black magic is in your own mind and *you* are the only one who can make it work or not. Mixtures of bat's blood, mandrake, human bones, cockerel feathers and other obnoxious things have no effect on anyone and are just disgusting concoctions.

Why is so much written in the press about black magic?

Because people like to read about it. There is some special fascination about eerie things, thus the popularity of horror films. Lurid stories of "black magic rites," sell newspapers. If journalists told the truth and said witchcraft was the remains of an ancient religion, people wouldn't be interested. (If this university had advertised that I was going to give a talk on the "old religion" and not on witchcraft, we wouldn't have had a packed house like we have tonight.)

Could Witches turn themselves into animals?

Of course they couldn't, but there are several explanations to account for this belief. Witches were full of fun and had a strong sense of humor. They were very unsophisticated and would join in all sorts of childish games. On their journey to the Sabbats, they often pretended to be animals and imitated the characteristics of the animals they represented. People seeing a group of witches playing these games would be only too ready to spread the tale that the witches had changed into animals.

Perhaps the witches dressed in animal skins to frighten the locals and prevent them from following and finding out where the meetings were held. Russell Thorndike, in his *Dr. Syn,* made the smugglers dress up as ghosts and demons to scare the people from the Dynchurch marshes when they were taking their smuggled goods through them on pack ponies. If smugglers did this sort of thing, the witches could have done the same. Animal skins would have been easy to obtain in those days, and in the dark they could easily be mistaken for the real thing.

Could Witches turn people into frogs and toads?

I don't know. It is quite possible that some of them could make a person believe he had been changed into a frog or toad, by hypnotism. I have seen stage hypnotists make people believe they were animals and have them crawling all over the stage, making animal noises. None of the audience believed they had changed into beasts, but the victims did.

I have read that Witches changed places with their familiars and went to Sabbats in the shape of a cat. Is this true?

It was believed that some witches took on the body of their cat and went to the Sabbats in this form, while the cat took on the witch's body and remained in bed. These stories were, most probably, started by the villagers. They would know the dates of the Sabbats and spy on some old woman who they believed to be a witch. Ten to one, the old woman wasn't a witch at all and had no intention of attending the Sabbat, but in the eyes of the locals she *was* one and would have to attend the meeting. They would see her put the cat out at night, which was the common thing to do, and believe the cat was the witch in disguise. An all night watch, through the window, would prove that the old woman remained in bed, so the spy would go back with the story that the witch and the cat had changed places.

Another explanation for this legend comes from the story of Diana, the Moon Goddess. Diana was in love with her brother Lucifer, who spurned her love. He always had a cat sleeping on his bed, so one night Diana changed into a cat and got into his bed. Then she changed back into her own form, and when Lucifer awoke he found a beautiful woman in his arms. When he found he had made love to his sister, he was furious and would have killed her, but Diana saved her life by charming him to sleep and exercised the first spell of witchcraft. Through this union, Diana gave birth to a daughter called Aradia, who was later, as the child of light and darkness, sent to Earth with the object of instructing mortals in the art of witchcraft.

It has also been said that people who wanted to rid themselves of someone they disliked, would catch a wolf and fix in its ears a pair of earrings stolen from their enemy. When the wolf was killed, the earrings would be discovered and recognized, and the owner would be destroyed for being a werewolf.

There are many stories of animals being shot at and a witch found bleeding to death in her own home. This could be true if witches dressed up in animal skins. Because so many lies were told about the witches, it is difficult to pick out the truth.

Do Witches use blood in their rites?

No. There was a belief that newly spilled blood gave off power. I have no idea how this idea started; perhaps it was just an excuse for killing. Witches make no use of blood in any of their ceremonies. Their rites are very beautiful and there is nothing very beautiful about blood. Neither do they sacrifice animals, birds or human beings. Because they belong to a fertility cult and worship a Goddess of Fertility, the killing of anything, except for food, would be entirely against their principles. They desire the production of life; not the destruction of it.

The whole idea of a sacrifice of anything, whether animal, bird, human or the products of the land seems pretty pointless, and I cannot see what it achieves. Neither the gods nor the worshipers get anything out of it and it is a sheer waste of life and crops; just destruction for destruction's sake. Anyone who worships the life-force in nature couldn't reconcile such a useless act.

Leaving food for the gods at the temples was an entirely different matter. This was invented by the priests who enjoyed a good meal after the worshipers had gone. Journalists who write about the sacrifice of a cockerel in witch-rites, should study their subject a little more. This has been borrowed from the voodoo religion, and I am not acquainted enough with the subject to know whether it is true or not. No doubt sensation-seeking writers have exaggerated voodoo as much as they have witchcraft.

Why do Witches work in a circle?

The circle represents the borderland between this world and the domains of the gods. Since it is a fertility cult, it also represents the womb of Mother Earth. The circle is nine feet in diameter. Some say it is the smallest space in which thirteen people can comfortably work; but I imagine the number has more to do with fertility. If the circle represents the womb, the nine feet could be connected with the number of months it takes an embryo to develop into a perfect child. It *could* be connected with the moon. It is also said that the dancing represents the quickening of the child in the womb and that the wild shouting represents the mother's cries in labor. Perhaps nine feet fitted into the average room of a house or cottage.

In the olden days, when lots of people attended the Sabbats in the open, the circle must have been a lot larger; perhaps some multiple of nine. I, personally, believe that on these big occasions, only those taking part in the actual rites entered the circle; the rest took their places outside like the congregation of a church.

Can you tell us anything about the rites held in the circle?

The high priestess first brushes out the circle with the broom; this is to make sure the circle is perfectly clean. Then she banishes all evil spirits from the area with the magical sword. Next, she draws the circle with the athame, or black-handled knife. Even if a circle is painted on the floor, she still has to draw it while reciting special words.

After this, she consecrates the water, and the salt which she mixes with the water. Then she lights the candles on the altar and those around the circle. This done, she purifies the circle by sprinkling the consecrated water around it. She also walks around the circle with the incense burner. Now the circle is ready to begin the meeting.

The priestess welcomes the other members into the circle and each one is purified with the holy water. All kneel while she offers a prayer to the deities, and with the sword, she invokes the gods to attend and help them with their rites.

If it is a special festival, the rites for that festival are then performed. Sometimes a new member is initiated or an old member is raised to a higher degree. After the rites, the members are asked if they wish to work magic to help anyone. If they do, this is discussed and the dance begins to raise the power. Then they all concentrate upon the person they hope to cure. That is why a photograph of the person is necessary.

Finally, they have a light ritual meal and the circle is closed.

Do Witches hold any meetings in churchyards?

Modern witches certainly do not, but in the early days, when Christianity and the old religion worked side by side, it is quite possible that some meetings were held in churchyards, as these places were used for all kinds of dances and festivities.

Churchyards might have been considered the ideal places to hold the Sabbats, because, in order to attract members of the old faith to the new one, many of the early churches were built in the sacred groves and on hills dedicated to the old gods.

Do Witches try to contact the dead?

They have no special rites or ceremonies for this purpose, but some modern witches are also interested in spiritualism and would use methods similar to those used by modern mediums. Dancing in the circle could work a person into a trance state, and if he was gifted with mediumistic powers, that would be the most likely time for him to make contact with departed spirits.

I, personally, have tried using a planchette and table-turning in the circle and have had very good results. Those they would most likely contact would be bygone witches and the old gods themselves.

Can anyone become a Witch?

Witches do not seek converts and no witch will ever ask you to join them. If you can find a coven that is willing to accept you and a high priestess who is willing to initiate you, then it is possible to become a member of the craft.

You cannot just walk up and join, there and then, as you would a society or club. The members must get to know you well, like you and consider you are a fit person to be a member of the craft. You will never be welcomed with open arms. You may feel that you are not wanted and that the members are trying to put you off. If you are easily put off by their attitude, they will know you are not really sincere and not a suitable person to be a witch. Covens that advertise for members, and high priestesses who are willing to initiate you right away, are *not* genuine.

As witches believe in reincarnation, they also believe that those who belonged to the craft in a previous life will finally find their way back to the circle.

What material gain would I get by being a Witch?

The answer is *none*. If you are trying to join the craft for material gain, you might as well forget all about it. You may receive spiritual enlightment, peace of mind and escape from the worries of this world for a short time, but witches are not interested in material things; even the help they are able to give others is given gratis with no thought of receiving anything in return. Perhaps that is why the old witches were poor people. They knew their reward would be in some future life. They could not even depend upon gifts from those they had helped, for they knew that human beings are very selfish and that once they have gained what they want, they forget all about those who have helped them.

Who is the head of the Witches in Britain?

There is no head of the witches. Each coven is complete in itself and governed by its own high priestess. No one can really say how many covens there are, as one coven doesn't know where the next one is and they have no connection with each other.

If a coven gets too big, a suitable member can be raised to the position of high priestess and start her own coven with those members who wish to go with her. There cannot be two covens within the radius of *three miles* from each other.

People write to me asking if I know a coven in their district. When I reply that I don't know, they usually think I am trying to conceal it from them. This is not the case. I really don't know. I may hear that one is functioning in some area, but I have no proof, and no means of contacting them.

Many witches do not like people to know they belong to the old faith. Whether they fear ridicule from their friends or persecution by the press, I don't know. I, personally, cannot understand why anyone should be ashamed of his beliefs. If more people admitted they were witches, the general public would soon begin to realize that all the stories of Satanism and orgies, written in the press, were a lot of lies.

Are all Witches female?

No. Witches are both male and female. In Scotland, sometimes, *male* witches were called warlocks.

From my study of the craft, I have come to the conclusion that witchcraft was originally a female cult. Being able to conceive children, which was considered the greatest feat of magic, woman was looked upon as the superior sex. She was the mother of the tribe, attended the sick, cooked the food and built the tents they lived in.

She took the chief part in the magic rites and the religious ceremonies. She is still the chief member of the coven, which she governs as the high priestess.

It was not until Christianity came to this country that men, as priests, took over the woman's part in the religious rites; even then they dressed in woman's attire, and the skirtlike costume of the modern priest is a throwback to those days. It is surprising that the majority of people who want to join modern covens are men. Many of those who join leave after a time, as they don't want to take orders from women, and try to start their own covens, making the high priest the chief character. This kind of behavior makes the craft a laughing stock to people who really know the true facts.

If I became a Witch would I have to give up being a Christian?

Witches are pagans and their religion is pre-Christian. We have no objection to anyone worshiping the old gods. The only objection might come from the Church itself. If one is satisfied with his own religion, I cannot see why he should want to join another. Personally, I cannot see how you can remain a Christian and also worship gods that your own church has turned into devils and demons.

Why shouldn't Christians be allowed to work magic?

I can't answer that one. You will have to ask your minister or priest. The only answer I can attempt is to suggest that because Christians believe their God is all-powerful, he doesn't require man's help; thus, the witches' ways of raising power would be of no use to the Christian. I suppose that masses of people praying could be considered a form of magic.

I have read that Witches used to grease their bodies with an ointment that acted as a drug and gave them the impression that they were flying. Is this true?

During the witch-trials, it was said that they used an ointment made from the fat of unbaptized infants, but this was obviously a story spread by the Church to encourage parents to have their babies baptized as early as possible.

Some writers have mentioned the use of drugs that might give the impression of flying. Dr. Margaret Murray, in her book, *The Witch Cult in Western Europe*, gives the following three formulae:

1. Parsley, water of aconite, poplar leaves and soot.
2. Water parsnip, sweet flag, cinquefoil, bat's blood, deadly-nightshade and oil.
3. Baby's fat, juice of water parsnip, aconite, cinquefoil, deadly-nightshade and soot.

She goes on to say: "I cannot say whether any of these drugs would produce the impression of flying, but I consider the use of aconite interesting in this respect. Irregular action of the heart in a person falling asleep produces the well-known sensation of falling through space, and it seems quite possible that the combination of a delirifacient like belladonna with a drug producing irregular action of the heart, like aconite, might produce the sensation of flying. The baby's fat and bat's blood would, of course, have no action."

Here is someone who has tried to explain how witches had the impression that they flew, but to me it is quite unneccessary. Why should anyone want to believe that he could fly? There would be nothing gained by using such drugs. Soot may have been used to make them invisible when they went to their Sabbats, in the same way that the Commandos blackened their hands and faces when they were on a raid. The oil would help spread the soot and keep it on their bodies, also grease on the bodies would give them a better chance of escaping if anyone tried to catch hold of them.

Do Witches send out missionaries?

They certainly do not. They don't even seek converts. They are very tolerant of all religions and think that each person should be allowed to choose his own god and way of worship. They do not understand why other religions should wish to convert everyone to their own way of thinking. Surely no one can believe that a god, who made the world and everyone in it, should choose one group more than any other, and condemn the rest to an everlasting Hell.

If you don't seek converts, why do you lecture on witchcraft and appear on television?

Because I think witches have suffered persecution long enough, and I wish to contradict all the lies that have been told about them. I want the general public to know the real truth about the craft.

Do television appearances help people to learn the truth?

Yes, if you can appear on a *live* show. If they are taped, it is not so good, as the producers can cut these tapes and almost make you say what they want you to. Most interviewers know very little about the subject and some try to belittle witches unless they know the subject and can hold their own. The best way would be to let a genuine witch give a short talk on her own, without constant interruptions from interviewers.

Why are black cats associated with Witches?

The true witches' cat is a "brindle." The old witches had to tame wild ones and these were brindles, like the Scottish wildcat of the present day.

They were merely used as pets, and some witches had toads, ducks or dogs. The legend of the witches' familiar was made up during the persecution days. Perhaps the black cat was introduced to make everything connected with witchcraft as black as possible. This may be the reason why the black cat is considered unlucky in America. Perhaps the fact that it is looked upon as a good omen in this country shows that the English weren't all against the witches.

Why is black associated with evil?

This is a case where your guess is as good as mine. I suppose it is because it is the color connected with funerals, but why this should be evil, I don't know, especially as Christians believe they go to heaven when they die. I can understand that black could be associated with sadness, but not with evil. Again it may be that because Christians use white as the emblem of purity, they naturally use its opposite for evil.

Do Witches believe in Hell?

No. The whole idea of burning forever in a blazing pit is very farfetched, and certainly doesn't tie up with a god of love. This idea was invented to frighten an uneducated people into being "good" and going to church.

How do Witches work magic?

They believe that nearly everything that happens was first conceived in someone's mind, therefore, if one wishes a person to do something for them, it is only necessary to change that person's mind in their favor. Providing that person isn't absolutely against the idea. It is often possible to do this by concentration. The late Dr. Gerald Gardner described it as a kind of long-distance hypnotism.

How could this be done?

This could be done by dancing in the circle to raise the power, and directing that power to the person's mind. All this takes a lot of physical and mental energy, but can be achieved with constant practice.

Can this power be used for healing?

Yes; providing one has a link with the patient and knows *exactly* what is wrong with him. All members of the coven must work together for the same result, as if they were one person. Unless they are in complete unison, they will never achieve any results. Some witches make a wax model of the person and concentrate on the exact spot of the body where the illness is.

Can a Witch do this on her own?

There are ways, but it would take a long time and a great deal of mental concentration.

Have you had any results?

Yes, many. One person we cured appeared with me on the David Jacob's Show, and said that if it hadn't been for my coven, he wouldn't be alive today!

How do you know the results haven't just been coincidences?

If a thing happens once or twice it might be

coincidence, but when it continually happens, coincidence is out of the question.

Could you work magic to make a person do something evil?

No. Magic works something like long-distance hypnotism; it would be the same as near-hypnotism, and no one can hypnotize a person to do something that is against his nature.

Could the power given off by the screaming "beatle" fans be used to work magic?

I not only think it *could* be used, but I think it *has* been used to raise the Beatles to fame and fortune. The teenagers, with their screaming, shouting and dancing, in a confined space, certainly raised the power. They unconsciously directed it toward the Beatles, as they had only these four boys in mind. The boys, naturally, desired fame and fortune, and with the masses working in their favor, they couldn't possibly fail.

I would say this is a very good example of modern magic. There have been better musicians that haven't got anywhere, simply because they hadn't that power behind them. Before these screaming fans were introduced, artists had to work very hard for many years before they became stars. Why should this sudden rise to stardom have only happened to people since mass hysteria became popular with the audience, unless it is magic?

Are there good and bad Witches?

I suppose there are, in the same way that there are good and bad Christians.

Do you believe in Christ?

Yes. I believe he was a witch. He worked miracles, or what we would call magic, cured people and did most things expected from a witch. He had his coven of thirteen. A high priestess, Mary Magdalane, who had been stoned as a witch, and he even finished his life as many of the old fertility gods did, knowing he was going to be killed. We know that the Church adapted many things from the old pagan faith, but it is unlikely that it should give Christ a coven of thirteen just to attract witches to the new religion.

Do Witches celebrate the black mass?

They certainly do not, and personally I doubt if it was ever performed. The idea was most probably invented by the Marquis de Sade in his book *Justine.* In any case, it was supposed to be performed by an unfrocked priest, and one would have to be a Christian before one could be that. It would be a useless thing to do and would achieve nothing. There is no doubt the idea has been commercialized and one can see a pantomime of it, at different places, if one has enough money.

You say the church has adapted many things from the old religion, Can you give me any examples?

I have already said how many churches were built on the sacred hills and in the sacred groves of the old religion. Sacred wells were turned into holy wells and dedicated to saints, where previously they were worshiped in honor of the old Celtic gods of stone and water.

The Derbyshire well-decorations is a case where it has persisted to the present day, although it has been Christianized and is now adorned with pictures from the bible made out of flower petals. Originally garlands of flowers were placed around the wells in honor of the old gods.

Bridget was one of the names of the Goddess; this was turned into Saint Bridget. Today, a girl who is about to be married is called a *bride* and for that day represents the Goddess of Fertility, and is expected to become a *mother* very soon.

The Last Supper could have been taken from an old witch ritual feast called "cakes and wine," and is the last rite performed in the circle.

Can a high priestess marry people?

There is an old witch rite, similar to a marriage ceremony, called "hand-fasting," which is just as binding among witches as a church marriage is to Christians. Hand-fasting would not be accepted in the eyes of the law, so witches who are bound together in the circle usually follow with a wedding at a registry office.

Do Witches forbid their members to attend the services of other religions?

No. If a witch wants to attend another religious service, it is entirely up to the witch to do as she wishes. As witches don't seek converts, they certainly don't fear that their members will join other faiths. If they wanted to, it would show they were not satisfied with witchcraft, and would therefore be better out of the circle. If more people attended services of other religions, it would make them more tolerant of other peoples' faiths.

In the old days, when people were forced to attend church, many witches gave lip service to Christianity, but worshiped the old gods in secret. Many saw the Virgin Mary as the Mother Goddess of the Old Religion.

Is it true that Christianity and the old religion once worked peacefully side by side?

Yes. It is also known that many priests and churchmen attended the Great Sabbats.

Crude carvings of the Goddess of Fertility, called Sheila-na-Gigs, and others, of the horned god, can still be found in old churches. These figures were not just put there by masons who were members of the old faith, and hidden out of sight. They are usually in very prominent positions and were not frowned upon by the clergy. The Lincoln Imp is a good example of this.

What does Sheila-na-Gigs mean?

This name is rather confusing. Some have translated it as The Lady of the Castle, others say it is The Lady of the Breasts, yet the late Dr. Margaret Murray points out that these figures have hardly any breasts at all and that the most prominent part is the sexual organ.

T. C. Lethbridge, in his book *Witches*, thinks the word was originally *Sithlach*, pronounced like Sheila and meaning "Holy Lady." He translates *na* as "of the," but does not accept *Gig* as meaning "breasts," which, he says, would have been *Keesh*. He assumes that *Gig* is a form of *Gog*, meaning "God," and the whole name would mean "Holy Lady of the God." This, no doubt, is the real meaning, and would be a very good description of the Goddess.

Is there a queen of the Witches?

I have already explained how every coven is a separate unit and is governed by its high priestess. In France she was sometimes called Queen of the Sabbat, and in Scotland, she was often known by the name, Queen of Elpham.

Do Witches believe in cremation?

Yes. It is much more hygenic than leaving a body to rot in the ground. As they believe in reincarnation, the old body is of no further use to them once they have passed over. They do not believe in a Day of Judgment when the dead will rise from their graves.

Many witches would like to be burned in the open, in the middle of one of the stone circles; but I'm afraid the local councils would object to this, although I can't see why a person can't be disposed of as he or she wishes. I suppose it is just another case of modern commercialism; the undertakers might object. I have often wondered what will happen in the future with so many East Indians in Britain; will we establish burning gnats?

The old form of burial was to curl the body up like an embryo in the prenatal position and return it to the womb of Mother Earth.

Has Herne the Hunter anything to do with Witches?

He was just another form of the old god. A man, dressed like him, used to appear in the old May Day celebrations. I presume he was the local god of a coven that met in Windsor Forest, and the meeting took place round the tree that was known as Herne's Oak. The remains of the tree was still there at the beginning of this century, but finally rotted away. He was supposed to appear at Windsor at the death of a sovereign, and this legend was obviously taken from the witches, as the old god was a god of hunting and death.

Edward III was a Plantaganet and a member of the old religion. He built a round tower at Windsor, known as the Devil's Tower, in which he is believed to have held witch rites, and was, no doubt the high priest of the Windsor coven. All this would account for Herne the Hunter being so closely associated with Windsor Castle.

Robin Hood was another form of the old god, and

the local deity of witches who met in Sherwood Forest, round the Major Oak.

Was Aleister Crowley a Witch?

No. Crowley was a magician who practiced abramelin magic. This was ritual magic, or "magick," as he spelled it to distinguish it from the magic of the conjurer. He once told my husband, Arnold, that he had been in the circle when he was young, but I very much doubt it. I think he said this because he didn't want someone to be what *he* wasn't. Besides, he once said he wouldn't take orders from any damn woman. If he was in the craft, he would have to take orders from the high priestess. This was rather against Crowley's makeup.

Do you believe Crowley was as "black" as he was painted?

No. I think he was a great student of the occult, a marvellous poet and he loved notoriety. He was very fond of women and attracted many undesirable people to him. His great fault was his drug habit and his biggest asset was his great sense of humor. He was born before his time. If he were alive today the general public would take little notice of him. At the worst, they would merely look upon him as an eccentric.

Do you believe that Joan of Arc was a Witch?

She was the witch of Domremy. It has been said that people ridiculed the Dauphin because he was put on the throne by a witch, so the Church finally canonized her and made her a saint. The reason why the peasants followed her was because they recognized her as a high ranking person of the old religion. It is said that she was convicted of heresy because she refused to accept Christ, but I think it was more political than that. A young girl who could gather the people to her side was too dangerous to be alive.

Many believe that she wasn't burned, and that someone else took her place on the pyre. This is probably correct as all roads were closed and none of the public were allowed near the burning. It is also said that later she married, had children and lived to a ripe old age.

What are the festivals observed by the Witches?

There are four major festivals: May Eve, August Eve, November Eve (or Halloween), and February 2. These correspond to the ancient Gaelic year, with its four fire festivals: (Samhain), Bridget, Beltâne and Lugnasadh.

The two summer festivals are in honor of the Goddess and the high priestess takes the principal part in the rites. The God is worshiped in the winter ceremonies and the high priest takes over. The high priestess can select anyone to be the high priest, providing he is of sufficient rank in the craft. In modern covens, he is usually the husband of the high priestess.

In the olden days, the chief of the clan or someone of great rank would take the part of the high priest at the Great Sabbats. This is the person that the Church called the Devil. It has been thought that some witches adopted this name for their high priest in order to scare outsiders and keep them from the meetings.

I wouldn't mind being a Witch, but I wouldn't like people to know. Could I become one under these conditions?

Yes; if you could find a coven to accept you. Most witches don't like "cloak-and-dagger" secrecy. One either wants to worship the old gods or one doesn't. If you are serious about it, you should have the courage of your own convictions and stand up for your beliefs. If you are scared of ridicule, it is better for you not to join the craft.

You say it is difficult to join the craft, yet I read of a reporter who joined a coven to expose the Witches.

So did I, but what kind of coven was it? There are many people nowadays who are trying to jump on the witchcraft bandwagon, who are not real witches at all. They are only too ready to initiate anyone for the sake of numbers. No genuine witch would initiate a person without knowing them for at least a year. The story that a reporter entered a genuine coven doesn't ring true, especially as he must have had a photographer with him to take the *photograph* of his initiation, *which appeared in the paper.* Don't tell me that all this went on without the witches knowing anything about it.

You say that there is no head of the Witches, but the papers must think differently. They mention queens and kings, and one man said he was the great Witch of Britain.

People can say anything, especially if they want publicity. People who want notoriety always use high sounding names; they believe it impresses others. In the latter part of the eighteenth century, a charlatan called Pinetti, who was really the son of an innkeeper, claimed he was a magician, and called himself a Knight of the German Order of Merit of Saint Philip, a professor of mathematics and natural philosophy, and a graduate of the Royal Academy of Science and Belles Lettres of Bordeaux. Another man, who went under the name of Comus II (his real name was Cotte), arrived at 22 Haymarket in 1793, and indulged in phraseology that would have puzzled the Greek professors at Oxford, for he talked about the "Enchanted Herologium, Pyxideen Literum and many curious operations in Rhabdology, Steganography and Phylacterin" as well as the "grand Dedecahedron" and "Chartomantic operations."

So far, witches haven't anyone up to these standards. It makes one believe in the old Chinese saying: "It is best for a man to keep his mouth shut and be thought a fool than to open it and remove all doubt."

Who was the last Witch to be burned in England?

This is a question that I am always being asked. Strange though it may seem, England never burned witches *under the law*. There have been one or two cases in which the villagers took the law into their own hands and burned the victim, but this was not legal. In England, witches were always hanged.

It is thought that the last witch execution took place in Exeter in March 1684. The name of the witch was Alicia Molland. Some writers have stated that witch executions took place in Northampton in 1705 and in Huntingdon in 1716.

The last person to be convicted of witchcraft was Jane Clerk, with her son and daughter, of Great Wigston in Leicestershire, in September 1717. The Grand Jury finally threw out the case.

In your studies, have you ever come across any cases of vampires?

No, and I doubt if there were such creatures except in fiction. Bram Stoker seemed to make the vampire popular when he wrote his book *DRACULA*. He was not the first Englishman to write fiction on this subject, and in the middle of the nineteenth century Thomas Preskett Prest wrote a book called *VARNEY THE VAMPIRE, or THE FEAST OF BLOOD*. He is perhaps better remembered for his play *SWEENY TODD, THE DEMON BARBER OF FLEET STREET*.

The only suggestion of a vampire dwelling in these islands comes from a history of England entitled *Historia Rerum Anglicarum*, written in the twelfth century by William of Newburgh, canon of the Augustinian priory in Yorkshire. He described how an evil man of Berwick, in Scotland, died, and how as soon as he was buried his corpse used to terrify the countryside by night, accompanied by a howling pack of demon dogs. The locals stayed in their houses and locked the doors to keep themselves free from the bloodsucking fiend. They believed that the air would become polluted from this night-walking corpse and bring about a plague, so ten young men, chosen for their bravery, were sent to dig up the grave and destroy the corpse. This they did by hacking it to pieces and burning it to ashes. Although this prevented the vampire from haunting the neighborhood, shortly afterward, Berwick had a plague which caused more deaths than in any other place in the country.

Recently, the newspapers reported that a young man had seen a vampire in Highgate cemetery, but it proved to be a hoax. No doubt he did it for publicity, as the story brought him an appearance on television!

Why did the church torture Witches?

The best way to answer this is to quote from some of the old books about the witch trials, as the Church had its own theory for torture. It asserted that the "attributes of God were true and were revealed to and by the Christian Church, who had the exclusive key to man's purpose in life and any other ideas were false and would not be tolerated. The Devil was always trying to set up a rival system and gain control. Anyone who supported the Devil was fighting the Christian God, who was the only true God." In A.D. 382, the Church declared that anyone convicted of opposition should be executed!

Witchcraft was considered a very grave crime as it was difficult to prove and no ordinary legal method could be used. To prove that someone was connected with the Devil could only be done by making that person confess, as the Devil would certainly not appear as a witness against his own supporter. Since working against the Church was working against God himself, it was treason and punishable by death. Because no human being would voluntarily confess to something that would cause his death, though it was supposed to be for his own good, he would have to be tortured until he confessed to his "crime."

When were Witches first executed?

Until the year 1200, witchcraft was looked upon as primitive magic and could only be punished in the civil courts by fines. When the Inquisition had put down most of the heretics, a search was started for new victims. It was decided that witchcraft could also be a heresy and proceedings were begun against fortune-telling and sorcery.

In 1320, Pope John XXII asked the inquisitors to destroy the Devil-worshipers. After that they declared that witchcraft *was* a heresy, and persecution against witches spread to the whole of Western Europe. The entire idea was fallacious because one must be a Christian before one can be a heretic, and witches have never been Christians. This was another case of pure commercialism; the property of the condemned witches could be confiscated, and many wealthy people belonged to the old religion.

Can you tell us some of the tortures used against Witches?

This is not a very pleasant subject, but I will.

The *Malleous Maleficarum* (or, The Witch Hammer), which was printed in 1486 gave the following method of examination by torture:

First, the jailer prepares the implements of torture, then he strips the prisoner. (If it be a woman, she has already been stripped by another woman, upright and of good report.) The stripping is lest some means of witchcraft may have been sewed into the clothing—such as often, taught by the Devil, they prepare from the bodies of unbaptized babies that they may forfeit salvation. And when the implements of torture have been prepared, the judge, both in person and through other good men, zealous in faith, tries to persuade the prisoner to confess the truth freely; but if he will not confess, he bids the attendants prepare the prisoner for the strappado or some other torture. The attendants obey forthwith, yet with feigned agitation. Then, at the prayer of some of those present, the prisoner is loosed again and is taken aside and once more persuaded to confess, being lead to believe that he will, in that case, not be put to death.

But, if neither by threat nor promises such as these the witch cannot be induced to speak the truth, then the jailer must carry out the sentence and torture the prisoner according to the accepted methods, with more or less severity as the delinquent's crime may demand. And while he is being tortured, he must be questioned on the articles of his accusation, and this frequently and persistently, beginning with the lighter charges—for he will more readily confess the lighter than the heavier."

This is the kind of hypocritical nonsense that was

written by these sadists, who delighted in torturing people and had no idea of letting any of their victims escape the penalty of death once they had been accused of witchcraft. Robert Burns certainly knew his fellow men when he wrote, "man's inhumanity to man."

Some female witches were raped by the torturer's assistant while they were being stripped, like Frau Peller, the wife of a court officer, in her trial at Rheinbach, Germany, in 1631. She was only accused of witchcraft because her sister refused to sleep with the witch judge, Franz Buirmann.

If, on her arrest, a witch confessed because she knew the kind of torture she would receive, she still had to undergo torture because it was held her first confession was falsely given to avoid the agony.

Here are some of the instruments used to obtain confessions from those accused of witchcraft at Bamberg, Germany, in 1627:

Thumb screws that were used with leg vises.
Flogging either off or while hanging on a ladder.
Stocks which had iron spikes. This torture was allowed to be carried on for as long as six hours.
Friction made by drawing a rope around the neck until it cut into the bone.
Immersion in cold water baths.
Holding burning feathers, dipped in sulfur, under the arms and groin.
The prisoner was made to kneel on a board with sharp wooden pegs. This was known as the prayer stool. Others were forcibly fed on herrings cooked in salt, and deprived of water and other liquid so that it caused a raging thirst.

The victim was placed in a scalding bath to which lime was added.

She could also be crushed in a vise or stretched on a rack, but this was not considered as a torture! After they were condemend to be burned, additional torture often took place, including cutting off their hands or tearing women's breasts with red-hot pincers.

There were various methods of burning. Some were tied to a stake, others were put in a straw hut or tied on a barrel of pitch. Some were tied to a ladder and slowly lowered into the fire. It is said that green wood, for slow burning, was used for impertinent witches. Others, before being burnt, had their limbs hacked off or their bodies were smashed on a wheel.

One must agree that these were strong methods for dealing with people who just wanted to worship their old gods, especially because the violence was perpetrated by those who taught that their own god was a god of *love!*

Not all churchmen believed in these confessions, and Bishop Hutchinson wrote in his *Historical Essay Concerning Witchcraft,* published in 1720:

Do but imagine a poor old creature, under all weakness and infirmities of old age, set like a fool in the middle of a room with the rabble of ten towns round about the house; then her legs tied cross, that all the weight of her body might rest upon her seat. By that means, after some hours, that the circulation of the blood would be much stopped, the sitting would be as painful as the wooden horse. Then she must continue in her pain four and twenty hours, without either sleep or meat, and since this was their ungodly way of trial, what wonder was it, if then they were weary of their lives, they confessed any tale that would please them, and many times they knew not what.

The Jesuit Friedrich von Spee asked in anger: "Now, in Heaven's name, I would like to know, since she who confesses and she who does not, both perish alive, how can anybody, no matter how innocent, escape?" He also states, "Perhaps the reason we are not *all* wizards, is the fact that we have not *all* been tortured."

One torturer's assistant is said to have boasted that he could make the Pope of Rome confess he was a wizard if he had him in the torture chamber.

Did Mathew Hopkins use these kind of tortures?

No. He invented tortures that would leave no marks on the bodies of his victims. His chief method was to walk them up and down for hours on end with no sleep. He also introduced the method of pricking, and spread the rumor that all witches had some spot on their body that would not bleed if pierced with a bodkin. He also used faked bodkins; some that were only sharp at one end. He would prod the witch with the blunt end, and then, by sleight-of-hand, turn the pin and insert the sharp end, so he could make blood appear, or not, as he desired. Other bodkins had a wooden handle, into which the pin slid so that it gave the illusion of entering the victim's flesh. Daggers made in the same way are used today in theatrical productions.

I have seen the film Witch-Finder General. *Was Hopkins killed as he was in the film?*

No. There were stories about him being swum as a witch, but this is not true. He began to accuse too many people of witchcraft, so that the authorities finally began to doubt his stories and refused to back him. He retired to his home in Manningtree, Norfolk, and died of tuberculosis about the year 1646.

It is said that mother Shipton was fathered by the devil. Could this be true?

The story in itself sounds impossible, but there is a reasonable explanation. If her mother was a witch and belonged to a coven, she could have had sexual intercourse with the high priest, whom the church called the Devil.

Why did witch-finders shave the Witches' heads and bodies before pricking them?

One reason is that the hair might conceal devil's marks, which were supposed to be marks put upon a new witch by the Devil, at her initiation. Also, witches were believed to have extra teats by which they suckled their familiars. Most of these marks were only warts and other skin blemishes.

Another belief was that the Devil might be lurking in the victim's hair and would tell her what to say at her confession; others thought that she might conceal amulets in her hair, while another suggestion is that the witches hair was her power, and if all hair was removed from her body, she would be powerless and have to confess the truth at her trial.

What were Beltane Fires?

In the central Highlands of Scotland, bonfires, known as Beltane Fires, were kindled with great ceremony on the first of May. Many famous writers have written about such fires, including the Scottish poet John Ramsay. He stated that on the night before the ceremony, all fires in the neighborhood were extinguished and next morning all the material for starting the sacred fire was prepared. A well-seasoned plank of oak was procured and a hole was bored in the center. A wimble of the same material was made and fitted into the hole, and the fire was started by friction. Three times three people were required to start the fire, and in other places, the number was three times nine. These were sacred numbers of the witch cult. It was believed that if any of these people were guilty of murder, adultery or theft, the fire would not kindle.

As soon as the friction produced sparks, a species of agaric, which grew on old birch trees and was very combustible, was added. This caused the fire to blaze up and shine over the countryside. The fire had many virtues and would cure all malignant diseases in humans and cattle.

Once the fire got going, the people used to sing and dance around it until it began to die down. Then a large cake called the "Beltane Cake" was brought forward, cut up and divided among the company. One particular part of this cake was called the "Beltane Carline"

(Scottish for "old hag"), and when the company found who had this piece, they lifted him in the air and pretended to throw him on the fire. Some people think that this mime proves that human sacrifices were once used. Any sick cattle were driven through the smoke and dying embers. Similar fires took place all over Europe. Others were lit on Halloween and around Christmas. The Yule Log is a throwback to the times when such fires were lighted. In some places the ashes of the Yule Log were scattered on the fields on the Twelfth Night. In other places, the log was removed from the fire as soon as it was charred and kept by the fireplace, ready to be put on the fire again whenever there was a thunder storm. It was believed that lightning never strikes a house in which a Yule Log is burning.

Need-fires were kindled at any time of the year for the purpose of achieving some special object. In the Middle Ages, the Church condemned them as pagan superstition.

What Women Want to Know

The following questions have been selected from those asked after lectures at Town Women's Guilds and other women's societies.

Could you make me a love charm?

Yes. There are numerous spells and love charms that have been used by different people all over the world, but, personally, I wouldn't make one myself. Love is a pretty chancy thing at times and unless a couple fall in love with each other, I doubt if it would lead to a happy married life. In the days when love charms and potions were popular, it was usually backed by a desire to physically possess a person; there was no thought of permanent marriage. If one person breaks off an engagement, there must be something wrong. A love potion or charm might bring them together again, but it might not be an advantage in the long run, and I doubt if it would be permanent. Personally, I would always be a bit wary of a man who had left me, and would always expect him to do it again. Maybe I'm not so trusting as a lot of women.

Are love charms used nowadays?

There must be a certain amount used, to judge by the number of such devices advertised in magazines. But I don't think they are so much in demand as they used to be, when it was very important for all girls to get married. This was for the sake of security, as there wasn't so much work that a woman could do. Modern life has changed all this and women can support themselves by doing almost all the jobs that men can do. I suppose the suffragettes, with their fight for the equality of the sexes, had more to do with the decline of love charms than any disbelief in magic.

Can you tell us about any of the love potions and charms used throughout the world?

To list all the different love charms would require a book, but I can give you a few examples, though some of them are rather revolting. Most of them required that the person desired should eat part of the body of the one seeking his love.

In some parts of Germany, a young woman would put a piece of sugar under her armpit and then drop it into the tea or coffee of her beloved. This, she believed, would cause him to be faithful to her.

In other parts of Germany, a piece of bread soaked in perspiration was allowed to dry and then was crumbled up in his food.

In Scandinavia, drops of perspiration were placed on an apple which was then pierced with a needle. It was considered a very potent love philter and is believed to have been taken from the story of Adam and Eve.

According to Gypsy-lore, a girl will take part of her clothes, which are thoroughly soaked with perspiration, add some hair from her armpits, burn it all to ashes, and mix it into the food of the man she loves. It has also been known for a man, at a dance, to wipe his left armpit with a handkerchief and then apply it to a girls forehead and neck.

In Wales, a love potion was made of mead, rhubarb, cowslip, primrose or elderberry wine. It was said that the person who drank this concoction would forget father, mother, heaven, earth, sun and moon and think of no one but the one who had made the mixture.

In Shropshire, a person could get a lover with a penny's worth of "dragon's blood." After cutting a piece of red flannel into the shape of a heart and sticking three pins into it, to represent Cupid's arrows, it had to be sprinkled with the dragon's blood and burned on the fire.

My grandmother told me that, in her youth, to make a husband who had left his wife return, a woman would catch a frog, put it in a bottle and bury it in the ground. When the frog had rotted away, the man would come back. Would this work?

This kind of spell was called "trash magic," and as long as the desire for the man's return is strong enough, there is no reason why it shouldn't work.

Skeptics would say that the majority of wayward husbands come back on their own accord, and that the destruction of the frog has nothing to do with it.

It is impossible to prove either way. Magic is so much like ordinary happenings and cannot be put on the dissecting table of the scientist. If the woman's husband returned, it could be coincidence; on the other hand, would he have returned if she hadn't buried the frog? Who knows? The only thing one can say on such matters is that if these old spells didn't work, why would they have persisted through the ages? Surely if they had failed they would have been rejected years ago, and other methods tried. There is no reasonable explanation for many old spells, and I, myself, have often wondered why people did such things; then, after trying them out, I have discovered that they do work, but I have no explanation why they should.

I presume Saint Christopher medals work the same way, or they, too, would have dropped out of fashion long since. I have heard of many people who swear they would have been killed if they hadn't possessed one of these medals. This is no easier to prove correct than the burial of the frog. One can only accept or reject the person's story. In both cases, the possession of these things turned out for the best, so does it really matter how it happened?

If I tried out a love potion, would it work for me?

There is no reason why it shouldn't work for you, as long as you desire that person's love sufficiently. Magic must never be done in a half-hearted manner. You must know what you want and really want it very much. It will take your desires *literally,* so it is not advisable to just play about with it or you may get more than you bargained for. In you really want someone's love, well and good; but you will have to accept him as he is, faults and all. You can't work magic to get a lover, and then, because he is not quite up to your expectations, work magic for another one. It just won't work. Make sure of what you really want, and if you really want it; then, if you still desire it, work magic to get it. If you are wavering, it is best to leave it alone, or you may get stuck with something you're not too keen on.

My father always wears a ring in the form of a snake, which he considers very lucky. Is this just his imagination, or is it an authentic lucky charm?

The serpent amulet dates back to the days of ancient Egypt. It represents the Supreme Being, and has come down through the ages to the present day. In many parts of the world, people wear serpent rings or bracelets, or carry about a replica of a snake as a protective charm. It is a phallic charm and is often used to obtain fertility.

I have heard of the "Hand of Glory." Can you tell me what it is?

The "hand of glory" was a charm mostly used by burglars. It was believed to cause a deep sleep to fall on the inhabitants of the house that was about to be robbed.

The person who wished to make one of these

charms had to creep up to a gallows, in the dead of night, and cut the hand off the murderer who hanged there.

The hand was wrapped in a piece of "winding sheet" and tightened until all the blood was drawn off. It was then placed in an earthenware bowl which contained brine of salt, black pepper and well-powdered brimstone. It was then left to pickle in this mixture for two weeks. When it was thoroughly dry, it was left in the sun to become completely parched. If it was made in winter, or at any time the sun wasn't very strong, it was dried in an oven heated by a mixture of vervain and fern.

There are various methods of using the hand. Sometimes, a candle, made from the fat of a hanged man, virgin wax and sesame was used, and the hand bent round it like a candle stick. Others braided wicks from the murderer's hair and dipped them in the special wax. These were attached to the fingers of the hand and lighted; the wrist acting as the base of the ghoulish candelabra. Anyone who was approached by this grim light was rendered incapable of any action.

Do you think this really worked?

If it didn't, I can't see why the robbers should spend so much time and trouble preparing the dreadful object. Hypnotism was most probably behind it. A frightened person, who already knew the reputation of the "hand of glory" would very easily react to its hypnotic power. Any bright object would have worked as well, but weird and uncanny objects were believed to be connected with black magic, and even today

certain people have a terror of anything that is supposed to be connected with it. Even people who don't
believe in it have a certain fear of anything connected
with a dead body. How many of you would walk
through a cemetery at night? Not many.

*You have told us that Witches use incense in their
rites. Is this the same as church incense?*

Some modern witches use church incense because
it is the easiest to obtain, and by this I don't mean that
they steal it from churches. It can be bought in any
Catholic repository. The ideal method is to use the
correct incense for the particular day on which the rite
is performed.

What are the incenses for the different days?

Every day of the week has its own incense, color
and perfume. Here is the list:

DAY	INCENSE	PERFUME	COLOR
Sunday	Mastic	Heliotrope	Orange
Monday	Myrtle	Wallflower	Violet
Tuesday	Aloes	Carnation or Pachouli	Red or Golden brown
Wednesday	Cinnamon	Sweetpea	Yellow or Gray
Thursday	Nutmeg	Stock or Lilac	Purple
Friday	Saffron	Apple Blossom	Light Blue or Emerald Green
Saturday	Pepperwort	Hyacinth	Dark Green or Brown

Do Witches use candles in their ceremonies?

Yes. Five candles are used in the witches' circle;
one at each point of the compass and one on the altar.

This last one is used so that the high priestess can see to read the rites.

Do you have to use the right colored candles for the various days?

This is not necessary; most witches just use ordinary white candles. Ritual candle burning was used by the American Negroes who practiced voodoo; and from the catalogues of the firms that supply occult paraphernalia, it appears to be a very complicated business. Different colored candles are used for different purposes, for example, red is for love, health and vigor; green for money matters; light blue for happiness and protection; and black for evil; and so forth.

Besides burning the correct colored candles for the desired purpose, one must also burn the astral colors for the one who is doing the rite and the one for whom it is being done. Astral colors are the colors for the zodiac signs under which the people are born: Aries is white, Taurus is red, and so on.

Besides this, each candle must be dressed, or rubbed, with a special oil for that particular candle. These oils are sold in bottles under numerous names: "Hi-Altar," "X X Double-Cross," "Lodestone," among many others.

Some of the rites require as many as sixteen different candles and the oils to go with them. Although these ceremonies are all accompanied by special psalm readings, they are not all what I should call *white* magic. To bring confusion to another; to arouse discord or anger or jealousy in another; to gain power over others; and to hex an enemy; these are certainly a dark shade of gray, if not altogether black.

All these candles can be supplied in the shape of crucifixes, human figures and even ancient priests in flowing robes. The prices are higher than for the ordinary candles, but they are said to be more effective. It seems a very expensive way of working magic, so perhaps that is why it has never been adopted by the witches.

Some witches used to scratch what they wanted to happen on a candle and then leave it burning on the altar. I am told this works.

Does a magician work magic the same as a Witch?

Witches have always kept to their old pagan gods, but the magician gave a Christian form to his magic by invoking the spirits in the name of God and his saints or angels.

They worked ritual magic which is also known by the names art magic and Cabalistic magic. This had its roots in the magical beliefs of ancient Egypt and Babylonia. The magician who practiced it believed he could call up great spirits, minor gods, demons or angels by means of long, complicated rites and conjurations, and command them to do his bidding.

Before he could do this, however, he had to know the names of the power that would enable him to invoke and control these beings. Everything had to be done at the right time, under the correct planets, and by using special working tools that had to be properly prepared and consecrated. If he did not do all these things properly, he might not be able to control the spirits who could cause him grievous bodily injuries or even death.

To become a magician was a very complicated process and required a great deal of education, with a knowledge of Latin and Hebrew to enable the magician to read the magical books or *Grimoires*, as they were called.

The paraphernalia, with its costly robes, swords, wands and pentacles, often of gold and silver, were very expensive, and it was only the rich that could indulge in this form of magic.

The church, for a long time allowed ceremonial magic, and many priests and churchmen practiced it themselves. It was also taught in many universities.

Was the magician's circle the same as that of the Witches?

No. The magician's circle was a very complicated affair. Two circles traced on the floor with names in Hebrew of the spirits that he wished to invoke written inside. Each circle was specially designed for the magician's particular purpose. Everything he used had to be purified and made of the special metal that would attract the spirit he wished to call up. Both magicians and witches have to take a ritual purifying bath, containing special herbs, before entering the circle.

The magician cannot leave his circle once he has entered it, until the spirit or demon is banished. His circle is a protection against these spirits or demons. The witch can enter and leave her circle whenever she pleases, as it is not a protection against demons; it is used to hold the power that she raises from the dance.

Witches do not conjure up demons, so a protection is quite unnecessary.

Are there magicians who work ritual magic today?

I suppose there are. I know of some who use Cabalistic magic, but I know very little about this. The last magician I knew to work Abra-Melin magic was Aleister Crowley.

Can they really invoke a demon?

I don't know. I imagine it is something like seeing visions in a crystal ball, which are really seen in the mind. There are several stories of people who have tried to conjure up a demon, and because they haven't done everything exactly as the *Grimoire* stated, they have been discovered, the next morning, dead, with an expression of terror on their faces. How true these stories are, I don't know. It is said that the magician must always be stronger than the demon he invokes. If he loses faith in himself and begins to get frightened, he is unable to control the demon and is destroyed by it.

Isn't this the same as a materialization in spiritualism?

The spiritualist doesn't command a spirit to appear. It is supposed to build up from ectoplasm, which is a peculiar substance that comes from the medium's own body. I cannot tell you any more about this, as I have never been lucky enough to see a materialization, so I have no personal proof that they really happen, though people tell me that they have witnessed this phenomenon.

Do Witches practice astrology?

Astrology has had no special connection with the witches, but I know some modern witches who are quite expert at it. The early witches, being very close to nature, would know the movements of the heavenly bodies and what to expect in connection with weather and crops. The moon was their most important celestial body, as they worshiped the Moon Goddess. The phases of the moon governed their meetings and Sabbats. It is still believed by some country folk that seeds planted at full moon give better results than those planted at any other time.

By a study of natural phenomena, a witch could predict rain, storms and fine weather, and was very useful to people, like farmers, who depended on such knowledge for their livelihood. Only the wealthy could afford to consult magicians, but witches had a rule that they must never accept money for their art, though they no doubt received gifts of food and other goods.

Because of their knowledge, during the days of persecution, witches became the scapegoats and were blamed for everything. They soon discovered that whatever you do, you will displease someone. If the crops were bad, through no fault of their own, *they* received the blame. If, by the use of their fertility magic, they were able to produce an abundance of corn, the market prices went down, and again they got the blame. If a person died, it was always through witchcraft. If they cured him by the use of their herbs, they were doing a doctor out of a job and the whole medical profession was against them. The witches just couldn't win.

Do Witches read tea cups?

Some modern witches may, but the old witches certainly didn't. Tea was much too expensive in those days. I should imagine it was a fairly modern convention; maybe early Victorian. It is slowly falling out of use through the introduction of tea bags.

Have the stone circles that one finds all over the country any connection with the old religion?

The worshipers of the old religion believed that the power used for working magic came from their bodies. De La Warr, in his book *New World Beyond The Atom*, describes this force as "resonance"—like electricity or magnetism—which will not work without some impulse given to it from the human body.

To speed up this force, the ancients did a frantic dance in a circle, and these stone circles were the places in which this dancing took place. The stones were put there with the idea of containing that power once it had been generated and prevented it from drifting away and being lost in the countryside.

It was thought that the gods could use this power and direct it to the required purpose. Men and gods had to work in harmony. Magic was considered necessary to obtain a good harvest and the fertility of cattle, so the dances took place at the time of planting the seeds and harvesting the crops. A Christianized version of the latter is the harvest festival. The time when the gods were thanked for their help.

Early man didn't just sow the seeds and hope for the best; he put his whole self into the effort to achieve good results. Similar acts of raising power are done today, like special days of prayer for some special purpose. Football fans also believe they can cause their own team to win by mass shouting. They add their own effort to that of the players. The only difference between this and the frantic dancing of the ancients is that in football there are fans working for both teams, whereas the ancients were all working for the same end.

Questions Asked
by Members of a
Psychical Research
Society

Who was the man in black one reads about in the Witch trials?

This was the person the Church described as the Devil. He would really have been the high priest of the coven. Although many covens were caught and the names of their members published, one never heard of the "man in black" being caught, although he must have been taken with the rest of the members. Some people think that the authorities never told outsiders who he was because they wanted the people to believe he really *was* the Devil and not to know that he was just a human being.

We know that, at certain festivals, when the God

takes over, the high priest performs the rites; if he is not present, the high priestess girds a sword around her waist, and plays his part. We also know that witchcraft was originally a woman's cult, so the high priestess must have always taken both parts. This may be the reason why the "man in black" was never discovered. The persecutors might have been looking for a *man* when they should have been looking for a *woman!*

In some of the old pictures of Witches' Sabbats, the leader is depicted as a devil with a goat's head. Is this just made up?

They could be, or they may have been drawn from hearsay from someone who had attended a Sabbat. It is believed that the leader often wore a goat's mask so that no one would know his real identity. Masks of the jackal-headed god Anubis were worn by ancient Egyptian priests, so why not by the witches?

Why would he want to keep his identity hidden from other members of the coven?

It wasn't only the members of the coven who attended the Great Sabbats; lots of townspeople and villagers also gathered there, something like a bank-holiday crowd. Often the leader was well-known or an important person who didn't want to be known by all and sundry. On the other hand, it might be as I have just said; this masked man really may have been a woman. In either case, the figure added a certain mystery to the proceedings.

When did witch-finders first start the idea of "swimming" their victims?

"Swimming" was a very ancient ordeal and goes back some thousands of years to the time of Babylon, about 2200 B.C. It was used against women accused of witchcraft and adultery, and was abolished in England in A.D. 1219, but was brought back again when the witch persecutions started, and was approved by James I, who wrote "Daemonologie." It was first used on the Northamptonshire witches in 1612 and later made good use of by Mathew Hopkins, the witch-finder general.

Is it true that King James changed his mind about Witches?

Yes. Toward the end of his reign he began to have scruples about what he had written and was inclined to believe that there were very few witches, if any at all.

How did they "swim" a Witch?

The witch was stripped and the right thumb was tied to the left toe. Then a rope was fastened around her waist and she was lowered into the water. If she sank, she was innocent; if she floated, she was declared guilty. The idea was that even water spurned a witch. Many innocent women were drowned because they were not pulled out quickly enough, and many appeared to float because those holding the rope held it tightly so they couldn't sink. This was done to prevent the witch-finders from losing their fees.

Are Spiritualists witches?

You'd better not let a Spiritualist hear that. Most Spiritualists claim to be Christians and Witches are pagans.

Can Witches contact the dead?

Yes, if a Witch has the powers of a medium.

A lot of Spiritualists are up in arms about the new Ouija Board that has been put on the market. Do you consider this harmful to those who are not mediums?

No. I have experimented with the Ouija Board for a number of years and I am convinced that it picks up things from the subconscious minds of the sitters. Very few things come through that are not known by at least one of the sitters. Also, it will not work if all the sitters close their eyes.

I don't know why there should be such an uproar about this old parlor trick, which used to be advertised in boys' magazines of the Victorian and Edwardian days, and was sold in the conjuring departments of the big stores.

To an outsider, any objection looks like "sour grapes" on the part of mediums who want a monopoly of these areas for themselves. The only objection I have is the price of the Board, which seems a lot for a thin piece of wood.

Do you believe that the American medium Estele Parks has succeeded in reading the sealed message left by Houdini?

I very much doubt it. In any case, it wouldn't prove very much to me. According to an article in the *Sunday Express*, the message was known to three people, including Dunninger, an American conjuror, so she might have picked up some information from *his* subconscious mind.

If I left a message, as Houdini did, I would have sealed it and put it in a bank, so that no one but myself knew the contents. Then it could have been opened after the medium had given her version of it. If it were correct, she would have read it by supernatural powers.

John Neville Maskelyne, the old English conjuror, soldered two slates together with a piece of chalk between them, and challenged any medium to materialize a message on the slates. Although he offered £1,000, no medium came forward and tried to do it. The slates are still in the Magic Circle Museum.

Do you believe that mediums can contact the dead?

Yes, but I don't think they can do this to order. It often takes a long time for us to get through to a person in this country by telephone, so I can't see how one can contact a person on another plane instantaneously as some mediums appear to do.

At some seances I have attended, the medium appears to be fishing around, hoping someone will accept the name they have given and so give them a lead. I must admit I have never seen anything very convincing.

Most people who attend seances are so eager to receive messages that they grab hold of the slightest clue, often supplying information that helps the medium.

Do you believe in ghosts?

Yes. I have had too many experiences myself and met too many people who have seen them to disbelieve in them.

What was the last case you came across?

It happened in my own home when a friend was staying with me. During the night, she came rushing into my bedroom, saying there was a woman standing by the dressing table in the room where she was sleeping. I went back with her but there was no one there.

She described how the woman was dressed and exactly what she looked like. Next morning, my mother recognized the description as that of my great-grandmother; after searching through a pile of old photographs, I found one of my great-grandmother, which my friend recognized as the woman she had seen. Although the photograph gave no idea of the height of the woman, my friend said she was very short; this fact was only known by my mother, as I had never seen her.

Questions from University Students

Is it true that prehistoric people had no idea that the male had anything to do with the production of life?

This is partly true and some primitive tribes have the same belief today. It was believed that the Moon was responsible for women becoming pregnant, and that man's function was to rupture the hymen so that the moonbeams, which were the real fertilizing agent, could enter.

Later, they believed that most women became pregnant through intercourse, but that certain babies were begotten by the Moon and had no mortal father. Such children were either royal babies or those predestined for some greatness. This is probably the origin of the legend of the Virgin-birth, which comes in the stories of many old pagan gods, and was retained by the Christians.

Women used to call on the Moon for help in childbirth, as the Moon was also believed to watch over the birth of the child. One of the duties of the midwife was to say prayers and make suitable offerings to the Moon—it was also thought to be the guardian and protector of women—in order to secure an easy delivery.

In the early days, all planting, cultivating and harvesting were womens' tasks, because they were under the guardianship of the Moon and had the power to make things grow.

The earliest way known to prevent pregnancy was for a woman to avoid exposure to moonlight or to rub spittle on her stomach to prevent it swelling. Some African women, today, refuse to sleep in the moonlight, and if they have to, will make sure they sleep on their stomachs.

Barren women used to lay in the light of the new moon and make offerings to it while it was waxing. Throughout the ages, charms, in the form of a crescent moon, were used to procure fertility in human beings, cattle and crops. Even today, many Catholic Italian women call the Virgin the Moon of the Church and address her as Mother Mary. Modern people still bow to the Moon and turn over the money in their pockets with the hope that it will increase.

Why is it bad luck to see the Moon through glass?

This is a modern relic from the days of the witches. If one saw it through glass, it showed they were not attending the Sabbath; they bowed to it in honor of the Moon Goddess and they held a silver coin because that was Her sacred metal.

*Had the waning Moon any significance to these peo-
ple?*

Yes. They thought the Moon was being eaten up
by some dark and destructive power, so the waning
Moon represented destruction and death. They considered this time to be extremely bad for any project,
especially that of sowing grain. It was also the time
when the powers of sorcery and black magic could be
invoked.

The belief in the power of the Moon was not only
realized by primitive people. Plutarch wrote that the
waxing Moon caused growth and increase and was of
good intent.

*We know the Moon has an effect upon the tides; is that
why Witches were thought to be able to cause storms?*

Rainmaking was one of the practices of the priestesses who served the Moon Goddess, and the memory
of this magical power survived into the Middle Ages
with the belief that witches could raise storms and
cause floods.

What was the Witches' caldron for?

The caldron was a fertility symbol and represented
the womb of the Great Mother. It was called the
"caldron of regeneration," and was of Celtic origin.

In the Middle Ages, the caldron was used for
brewing what was known as "medicine" magic. When
the potion was brewed it was thrown over the fields to
secure a good harvest, or thrown in the air to cause

rain. It has been stated that the reason witchcraft persisted in spite of the terrible tortures and burnings was the fact that women who took part in witch practices believed that the fertility of the country depended upon their activities. It has also been suggested that the Holy Grail of the Arthurian legends is a Christianized version of the Celtic caldron.

Who was the Goddess of the Moon?

The Moon Goddess was known by numerous names in many different countries. In early days, the Moon was represented by the Goddess Selene. Later, she was replaced by Aphrodite, the bright moon, and Hecate, the dark moon. Later still, there were three goddesses, Artemis, Selene and Hecate. She was sometimes called Hecate-the-three-headed. She represented the three phases of the moon: Artemis was the crescent or waxing moon, Selene the full Moon and Hecate the waning Moon.

The Greeks represented the power of the Moon by Hecate the dark Moon, and her rites were performed by night. She was the giver of inspiration and understanding, and was the Goddess of Magic and Magicians. On the negative side, she was responsible for lunacy, which takes its name from Luna, the Moon.

Since you belong to a fertility cult, what is your reaction to the Pill?

Having babies isn't the only thing that comes under the term "fertility." Crops, cattle and vegetation also fall within this heading.

I have no objection to the Pill, providing one can

be certain enough research has gone into its making, and that there are no ill aftereffects. I wouldn't consider it perfect as it remains today. The way the population is growing, it is obvious something must be done to discourage overpopulation, but why should the woman always be the one who has to bear the brunt of these new discoveries? What is wrong with the old forms of contraceptives?

It is pretty certain that prehistoric man wasn't all that keen on large families; food was not very plentiful; and hunting, to survive, was not at all easy, especially with the primitive weapons they had.

The fact that they were accustomed to nudity, would have lowered the sexual urge; and, of course, the span of life was much shorter then. If the sexual aspect of everything wasn't so heavily advertised, perhaps the modern generation would settle down to a more sober life. As it is, sex leers down at you from billboards, cinema screens and television. One can't get away from it. No doubt the scales will even themselves in time, or "familiarity will breed contempt."

Is it true that Witches perform their rituals naked?

Yes; like many of the ancient worshipers, witches keep to religious nudity. They are taught that they must enter the circle as they come from the womb.

Don't you think that this causes outsiders to imagine Witches indulge in sexual orgies?

The true Witches are not interested in what the outsiders imagine; the custom of performing their rites in the nude comes down from ancient times, so why should it be altered for the sake of a few narrow-minded people who know nothing about the craft?

The Witches know that no orgies take place in their rites, but no amount of talking will convince people that such things don't happen if they have already made up their minds to believe otherwise.

There are plenty of nudist camps in this country, so if you believe that nudity raises the sexual urge, you should visit one. You would soon alter your opinion and discover that complete nudity is the most antisexual state there is. Early man and many tribes discovered this, and had to cover themselves with tattoos, ornaments and finally clothes, to attract the opposite sex.

Why should one go into a magic circle and perform rituals just for the sake of sex? Wouldn't it be far better to join the Hippies and attend one of their love-ins?

What does Pagan mean?

The word *Pagan* is from the Latin *Paganus,* meaning "peasant," or one who lives in a village. The word *Heathen* is Anglo-Saxon and just means "a dweller on the heath."

How could they hold nude out-of-doors ceremonies in an English climate?

They always lit a bonfire, which they danced around. When the weather was too bad, they would hold their meetings in barns.

Do you believe that the ancients used the same rites as the modern witches?

I think that basically they were the same, but many things must have been added or altered through the ages. During the days of persecution, when the craft went underground, a lot must have been lost, as information was handed down by word of mouth because most of the early people were unable to read or write.

If the Witches went underground, why were so many executed?

I think that a great many of the old women who were hanged or burned were not witches at all, but only old women who were disliked by the villagers. The witch-hunts opened up an easy way for people to get rid of those they hated. One had only to denounce someone as a witch and the chances were good that she would finish up on the gallows.

As the torturers made convicted witches denounce others, some genuine witches must have been taken as well.

Can you give us an example of an ancient rite?

It is pretty obvious that the earliest initiations took place in caves. The new member had to go through a ritual that symbolized the sex act so she would be "reborn" into the craft.

If anyone has visited Wookey Hole Cave, in Somerset, he will see the kind of cave that was used. As we know, there was a "Witch of Wookey"; her magic crystal ball has been found in the cave with her skeleton, and it is likely that this was a cave of initiation. Caves always represented the womb of the Great Mother, and hills represented her breasts. Hence—Mother Earth.

The Wookey Hole Cave is a perfect representation of the female sex organ, having a long passage that leads into a large chamber—the womb.

The ancient witches would carry the initiate (while others formed a procession behind) and take her into the chamber. This act symbolized the male seed penetrating into the female. There she was left, tied up in the prenatal position, and remained for a number of hours, or days, which corresponded to the number of months that it took for the embryo to grow into a fully developed child.

In this dark cavern, the initiate underwent an ordeal of fear, as she thought of all the horrible things that might happen to her; death from attacks by wild beasts, or from terror.

After the allotted time had elapsed, the rest of the coven would enter the cave, carrying torches, and would cut the vine with which she was tied ("the umbilical cord"); she was lead out into the daylight as a new "Child of the Goddess," and given a ritual bath in a nearby stream. Most of these ancient rites were in mime and very few words were spoken. Actions would mean much more than words to these primitive people.

It may be that this ancient symbolic rite later gave rise to the stories that witches performed ritual copulation in their ceremonies.

Do all modern covens use the same rites?

This is impossible to know unless one has visited them all. I imagine they differ to a certain extent in the same way that rites in Masonic Lodges differ. There are great differences in the services of different denominations of the Christian Church; and the same applies to Buddhism.

Why was there no mention of the Goddess in the Witch trials?

There is no real evidence that she wasn't mentioned, as all the reports that have come down to us were written to give witchcraft the worst image. The courts could suppress anything they wanted to conceal. It has often been said that convicted witches only said what was put into their mouths by the inquisitors, and even then, there is no proof that the devil they spoke of was anything more than an ordinary man in costume.

Perhaps the Church ignored the Goddess because it could not change her into a female demon, as they had done with the Horned God. The nearest figure the Church could have equated with the Mother Goddess was the *Virgin Mary,* and this certainly would not have suited its purpose.

Witches must have been evil, or the Church wouldn't have condemned them.

This is not true. Witches were condemned because they were rivals to the established Church and had to be made as black as possible. This was propaganda, in the same way that newspapers and cartoonists make an enemy of our country look worse than it really is.

One gets tired of this continual talk of evil. Anything that is not in line with the "establishment" is considered evil, though it may be ultimately for the good. The Church once condemned surgery and even baths; both have long since been recognized as good for the community.

Many of the old witches were the medical practitioners of the day and cured people with their herbal remedies; many of which have since been incorporated into modern medicine.

One must consider the early witches in a sensible manner. Why should these women spend their lives doing evil? What could they have gained by it? It was said they killed people by sticking pins into wax images; caused cows to become dry; raised storms and blighted crops and cattle; but we also know that all these things are impossible.

What is a Satanist?

In the Old Testament, Satan was not intended to be one person. The word *Satan* comes from the Hebrew and means "adversary"—it was just an opponent. I therefore think a Satanist was an opponent of the orthodox religion.

There are supposed to be people who worship the Devil, but I have never met one. I suppose they descended from the Gnostics who looked upon Satan as a god equal to the Christian God. They believed that Satan ruled this world and God was far away in some other sphere. They considered this world to be Hell.

There are lots of people who think the same today, but they are neither Satanists nor Gnostics.

Have you ever met a Satanist?

I have met two people who claim they are Satanists. Both were insignificant men who had no power at all, and only desired publicity for their own egos. Such people usually have an inferiority complex and have to boost themselves up somehow.

Then you don't believe that black magic could hurt you?

You are quite right, I don't. You can stick pins into a wax figure of me to your heart's content and it won't do me the slightest harm.

Some modern writers still believe in the evil of witchcraft and do not accept Dr. Murray's theory that it is the remains of an old, pagan religion.

These are usually strict Christian writers who want to maintain the evil image of witches. Their books are usually full of quotations from the old witch trials and in their bibliographies they never list any books by prowitch writers or by witches themselves, though they must have read these books.

It would not be to their advantage to believe the "Murray theory," as this would show that the witches were *pagans* who had been wrongly convicted by the Church as *heretics*.

Doesn't the Bible say, "thou shalt not suffer a witch to live?"

This is the question that I am always being asked by antiwitch people, so I have the answer already prepared.

The Hebrew word *Kaskagh* occurs twelve times in the Old Testament, with various meanings.

Reginald Scot pointed out, in 1584, that in that particular case, it meant "poisoner," and certainly had nothing to do with the highly sophisticated Christian conception of a witch.

He also stated, "The numerous Hebrew words, uniformly translated *veneficus, maleficus* or *witch*, covered many different practitioners of the occult, from jugglers to astrologers. To refer to all these different classes by one word (witch) is inadequate and erroneous."

Thomas Ady, who also tried to expose the witchcraft superstition, wrote: "The definition of *witch* based on the pact with Satan, transvection, metamorphosis, Sabbath and maleficia was neither implied nor defined in the Bible. That the Old Testament did not deal with witchcraft is hardly surprising, for witchcraft depended on a Christian demonology."

Sir Walter Scott, in his *Letters on Demonology and Witchcraft* wrote : "It cannot be said that, in any part of the sacred volume, a text occurs indicating the existence of witchcraft, under the Jewish dispensation, in any respect similar to that against which the lawbooks of so many European nations have, 'till very lately denounced punishment. . . In the Four Gospels, the word, under any sense, does not occur!"

Yet these mistranslations caused the untimely death of thousands of innocent people.

Would you like to see the old religion take over from the Christians?

No. I am quite satisfied to let everyone worship his own god in the way he wants to, and I wish to carry on with my own religion without others condemning it as something evil when they know nothing about it.

It would be impossible for a country to change its religion unless conversion started from the top, beginning with the sovereign. This is the way Christianity established itself.

Don't you think that by reviving an old religion you are setting the clock back?

The renaissance of the old religion is in no way setting the clock back; most religions of truth are as alive today as they ever were. The people of ancient Britain were as much, if not more, advanced than the present-day person as regards spirituality, and they had much more faith in the afterlife. The worship of nature, and the forces behind it and the universe, is essential if one is to be in tune with one's self and life generally.

The cycles in nature and man show that applications of these laws are only commonsense, and can aid man in his works if he will but heed them.

Bibliography

This brief Bibliography is to help readers in finding books Witches themselves recommend. For a fuller listing see Dr. Martello's *Witchcraft: The Old Religion* which contains a six-page Bibliography.

Anderson, Victor, *Thorns of the Blood Rose*, Cora Anderson, San Leandro, Cal., 1970

Buchanan, Dr. J. R., *A Manual Of Psychometry*, Boston, Mass., 1885

Buckland, Raymond, *The Tree*, Samuel Weiser, Inc., New York, 1974

Buckland, Raymond, *Witchcraft From The Inside*, Llewellyn Pubs., St. Paul, Minn., 1971

Crowther, Patricia and Arnold, *The Witches Speak*, Athol Pubs., Isle Of Man, 1965

Crowther, Patricia, *Witchcraft In Yorkshire*, Dalesman Books, Yorkshire, England, 1973

Crowther, Patricia, *Witch Blood: Autobiography of a Witch High Priestess*, H-C Publishers, New York, 1973

Farrar, Stewart, *What Witches Do*, Coward McCann and Geoghegan, New York, 1971

Frazer, Sir James G., *The Golden Bough*, Macmillan Company, New York, 1958

Gardner, Gerald B., *Witchcraft Today*, Citadel Press, Secaucus, New Jersey, 1955

Gardner, Gerald B., *Meaning of Witchcraft*, Aquarian Press, London, 1959

Glass, Justine, *Witchcraft: The Sixth Sense*, Neville Spearman, London, 1965

Graves, Robert, *The White Goddess*, Noonday Press, New York, 1966

Leland, Charles Godfrey, *Aradia, or Gospel of the Witches*, David Butt, London, 1899; Dr. Martello, New York, 1971

Leland, Charles Godfrey, *The Mystic Will*, Dr. Martello, New York, 1972

Lethbridge, T. C., *Witches*, Citadel Press, Secaucus, New Jersey, 1972

Martello, Dr. Leo Louis, *Witchcraft: The Old Religion*, University Press, Secaucus, New Jersey, 1973

Martello, Dr. Leo Louis, *What It Means To Be A Witch*, Hero Press, New York, 1974

Martello, Dr. Leo Louis, *Witches Liberation and Guide to Covens*, Hero Press, New York, 1973

Martello, Dr. Leo Louis, *Curses In Verses*, Hero Press, New York, 1971

Martello, Dr. Leo Louis, *Black Magic, Satanism and Voodoo*, H-C Publishers, New York, 1972

Martello, Dr. Leo Louis, *Hidden World of Hypnotism*, H-C Publishers, New York, 1969

Martello, Dr. Leo Louis, ed., *Witchcraft Digest*, Nos. 1 and 2, New York, 1973

Martello, Dr. Leo Louis, ed., *Wica Newsletter*, Nos. 1 to 30, New York, 1970–1974

MacCulloch, J. A., *The Religion of the Ancient Celts*, T. and T. Clark, Edinburgh, 1911

Murray, Margaret A., *Witch Cult in Western Europe*, Oxford University Press, London, 1921

Murray, Margaret A., *The God of the Witches*, Daimon Press, Essex, England, 1962

Shah, Idries, *The Sufis*, Doubleday and Company, New York, 1964

Valiente, Doreen, *Where Witchcraft Lives*, Aquarian Press, London, 1962
Valiente, Doreen, *An ABC of Witchcraft*, St. Martin's Press, New York, 1973